Welcome

In our home growing up Dad's mineral collection was as constant as the man himself -- steady in the background and too often underappreciated by his children. Fifty years later, it's time to set the record straight. The collection is amazing and the man is pretty cool too.

When my parents made the difficult decision to downsize from their spacious condominium, the six glass cabinets of carefully curated minerals needed a new home. It took many weeks, but eventually the display collection was relocated to my home. Dad seems at peace with the separation, but I'm sure he misses "his friends." When he comes to our house, he'll often disappear into my office where the collection is now, just to say hello to them.

There was something about moving his minerals into my house that sparked in me a new interest in my father's lifelong hobby. I developed a fresh appreciation for the collection — not unlike, perhaps, the way we adult children develop a new appreciation for our own parents as we age. I began to think that more people ought to see this. It's too beautiful to hide away in my office.

1955

In the Fall of 2024, I bought a small lightbox and began taking pictures of the specimens. They turned out better than I dared hope. I began reading and asking questions. I learned the difference between a silicate and a carbonate, why galena is so heavy, and why the sulfur couldn't be kept with the other elemental specimens where it logically belongs. As often happens, the more I learned, the more I wanted to know. In some ways, this book documents my own mineralogical education. Dad already knew all this stuff.

1974

The pictures speak for themselves. They are beautiful, and if that's all you're interested in, please enjoy. You'll notice a sprinkling of chemistry throughout the book. If you find chemistry as off-putting as my Mom does, you can blame me for its inclusion. (She still holds organic chemistry responsible for making her change her major in college.) If you're like me, though, you may find that a little bit of chemistry adds to your appreciation of the photographs.

Dad was concerned this book project was going to take a long time. I'm writing these words here at the project's end, and honestly, I'm a little sad it's done. As a record of Milt Leet's lifelong enthusiasm for a beautiful hobby, this project has been fascinating. As an enriching, shared connection with my Dad, it's been priceless.

— Tim Leet

2012

"much to our amazement"

The moments from your childhood when you feel like you are truly special are some of the most memorable. In this memory, I did nothing to earn this status. I just had a great Dad with a hobby that 5- and 6-year-olds thought was super cool. It must have been cool. Why else would the elementary school load up a bus full of kindergarten students for a field trip and transport them to the basement of my house? I do remember feeling very important as I stood next to my dad and he asked my classmates, "Which rock do you think is heavier"? He pointed to a very large rock and another that was much smaller. Of course, we all agreed the larger rock must be heavier. Then, much to our amazement, the rocks were passed around and it was the smaller rock that had to be hefted around the circle. My father entertained us with stories about mining and the treasures you can unearth. He presented his personal treasure trove that sat in glass cases and used impressive words like gypsum, fluorite and quartz. The card table was full of minerals we could all touch and pass around. My Dad, being a showman at heart, saved the most awe-inspiring presentation for the end of our expedition. My classmates gazed upon a drawer full of what appeared to be nothing more than rocks from our garden. My anticipation soared as my Dad turned off the lights and waved his magic wand over the rocks. The rocks began to glow in pink, blue, green and yellow. The UV light he waved over the rocks displayed a rainbow of fluorescents and we all gasped in delight. Over the years, the mineral cases were no more than another piece of household furniture to me. They were always there. But it never failed to amaze my friends when they would come over to visit and discover the gems hidden away in our basement.

-- Julie (Leet) Combs

1975

The Seeds – The Growth – The Results

Written in 1998, this is the story of how I got my start.

The year was 1950. A neighbor had returned from the shores of Lake Superior to my home town of Grand Rapids, Michigan. He had with him some stones washed ashore and worn into smooth, rounded objects. What appealed to me was the variety of color. I had no idea rocks came in such a variety of colors. Much to my dismay, a search of the local surroundings of the neighborhood offered no such "gems". Instead, there were some fossils. These were not nearly as appealing, but they were interesting.

Moving to the farm lands of Illinois did nothing to pique my interest in minerals, but then we traveled west, and along the roads were Rock Shops. It was at these locations that I was truly awakened to the beauty of minerals. My exposure was very limited but long enough to awaken a desire to collect again. This time my sights were set higher. I knew what I could afford, and I knew that time was on my side. As a high school student, I had a lifetime to pursue collecting. After completion of high school, I entered Missouri School of Mines to pursue a degree in mining engineering. The summers of 1960 and 1961 found me in the west working for Climax Molybdenum and Phelps Dodge.

Upon the completion of college, I was offered a job with Bethlehem Steel. Bethlehem had two iron mining locations in Pennsylvania. I spent 15 years working at these mines. In that time, I conducted many college field trips through the operations. On one occasion, Art Montgomery visited with his group from LaFayette College. Art, like a few others at various times in my life, rekindled my interest in improving my collection. Leighton Donely, a shift boss, was another individual who contributed to a rebirth of my desire to improve the collection. He had a display which I liked. Individual specimens were mounted on Styrofoam with a beveled front edge where an identification was mounted by two straight pins set in the Styrofoam. The great advantage of this was the ability to show the specimen in the best possible position in a secure "nest" cut into the top of the Styrofoam which conformed to the shape of the bottom of the specimen. I copied his display manner and acquired a large, glass, floor-mounted display case for specimens. I was in Cornwall, Pa. at the time.

The year was 1967 and the collector in me had come out of the closet again. This time I turned my attention to displaying in the base cabinet and one Wadell case acquired in high school. This Wadell case had found a place in my parents' front room in college and in the dining room when I worked at Cornwall. The floor case was relegated to the basement. Also, finding its way to my basement was an old blue print file that the mines had converted into a mineral cabinet. These compartmentalized drawers housed specimens up to 3x4x4 with some 3x6x6. The point of this is to explain why I have never been interested in collecting specimens which will not fit in these drawers. I have always believed that specimens kept in boxes were of no use to anyone. If they cannot be seen with relative ease, they are not worth having.

Before having to leave the Cornwall mines in 1972, I spent some time in an old collecting area that had brought growth to Leighton Donely's collection in years past. It was an area in #3 Mine that had not been mined, but slushing drifts and window cutouts had been made. This development revealed natrolite, apophyllite and analcite in the diabase. The interesting thing about these mineral occurrences was the variety of crystal forms. The crystals were clear to white and set on the dark diabase rock which made appealing specimens. I went back to these old workings and extracted enough specimens to trade. Up until that time, I had merely collected for myself. Now I was collecting for others, and as a result, my own collection grew in size and variety. Had that mine not closed, forcing me to move, I would have had a much larger collection today. For once I did something for myself and not the company. It was a very rewarding experience.

From 1972 through much of 1977, I worked in Bethlehem's Grace Mine in Morgantown, Pa. Here, there were large dodecahedron crystals of magnetite in a weathered white antigorite. This location was available; but with the exception of only a few occasions, I did not take advantage of using it as a trading source.

While at Morgantown, I added two Wadell cases which were mounted on top of the large floor case. In early 1978, I left the mining world. Well, I almost left the mining world. I went to work in Cleveland, Ohio, for General Electric. They wanted a mining engineer to look after two properties in the west where they owned sources for the making of tungsten filament wire for light bulbs. I visited those sources as well as some other mineral properties where they had interests. This was a rather short -- less than three years -- venture for me.

At the end of 1980 I completely lost contact with the mining world - with a few exceptions. As a result of the demise of my working at a source of mineral specimens, I have become more reliant upon purchasing instead of trading for minerals. This has not been all bad. As is the case with all growing collections, housing a collection becomes a problem in time. Three more Wadell cases were added and the floor case was disposed of when we moved to Ohio in 1978. The Wadell cases were arranged in a wall mounted setting in the basement in Ohio. Over the 20 years since that time, the size of the display has not increased. What has increased is the quality of the specimens on display. The old, converted blue print cabinet is still with me. It is in the basement while the Wadell cases finally found their way upstairs when we moved to Louisville. By that time the children were out of the house, so there was a place for them. It is a converted bedroom. I call it my den. It's a great thing to be able to sit here at this computer and see these "Friends of Mine". Some of you may remember the poem I wrote about them which appeared in an earlier issue of The Kyana Gemscoop. There are about 250 specimens which adorn a wall area 9 feet wide and 6 feet high. There are 34 glass shelves each 3 feet long, 4 inches high and 6 inches deep. The mirror backed, glass sliding doors on the cases expose all facets of each specimen to the eye. The specimens are grouped into chemical families. This does not give the best aesthetic presentation, but it does create some sense of order to the display.

There are 6 cases. One case has zeolites and associated minerals, another has carbonates, another silicates, and yet another has personally collected specimens from the mines where I worked in Pennsylvania. The other two cases have shelves devoted to metallics, native elements, barites, celestites, fluorites, sulfates, wulfenites, vanadinites, mimetites and others. The case in the basement is arranged chemically also for the most part. There is a drawer of self-collected zeolites and associations from Cornwall, a drawer of other zeolites, and a drawer of other Cornwall minerals. That drawer was the idea of Art Montgomery. I still remember him telling me that collecting a representative group of minerals from this location was a worthwhile thing to do. There is a drawer of silicates, carbonates, metallics, fluorescents, miniatures, specimens from Grace Mine, and cabinet specimens. About 800 specimens are in those drawers.

Friends of Mine

A special thanks to some friends of mine.
Some are dull and others shine.
Their colors are pretty and they are varied in form.
I have no idea of when they were born.
Some have been with me for many a year.
And I was thinking you would like to hear
About a few families and friends of mine,
And that is why I am writing these lines.
There are some friends who grew up alone.
They never had companions or much of a home.
They are the elements - proud and bold:
Copper and sulfur and silver and gold.
Some individuals I am sure you know
Because they have a colorful glow.
Lead is present in all these friends:
The mimets and crocos and vanadins and wulfens.
Two individuals I place in this group
Have elemental differences with the troop.
The absence of lead is their plight.
They are adam and vivian with the last name ite.
Some individuals in a group all alone
Are those who belong to the fluorite home.
They appear in such beautiful hues
Of brown, yellow, purple, greens and blues.
Those who guard these friends of mine
Form a group called the metallic line.
Here oxides and sulfides make a bed
With antimony, iron, zinc and lead.
Most of my friends are in the family of ates.
They are carbonates, sulphates and silicates.
These families unite in a negative way-
Some dark as night and some bright as day.
Sulphates have two in the variety show.
Each is quite nice and all aglow.
Some dressed in colors: white, gray and brown
While others dress in a see-through gown.
These sulphates are the barite and selenite twins.
Each strike a glow for the camera lens.
Another is celestite in various shades of blue –
Making them popular with quite a few.
Carbonates come in colors so warm,
And there is such an abundance of form:
From the delicate, white aragonite tips
To calcite peaks and dolomite dips.
There is cerrusite in all forms and shapes,
And the bumps on smithsonite look like grapes.
There are malachite greens and azurite blue,
Pinks of dolomite and rhodochrosite, too.
Many calcites live in this place,
And each one has a different face.
Though all of them have but one name,
Their forms and colors are not the same.
Silicates are the favorite of mine.
Quartz has a clean, crystalline line.
It is a very attractive target,
As is tourmaline, feldspar and garnet.
Silicates also have others to thank
For giving them their number one rank:
Hemimorphite; byssotite, pyrophyllite too –
Dioptase and rhodonite to name but a few.
Some silicates have a zeolite blend.
Soft colors and fragile forms, they lend.
The thing I like most in this neighborhood though
Is the close associations they make as they grow.
Sprays of natrolite, pectolite and messolite are here.
Bold shapes and meek bumps also appear.
There are colors of green phrenite and stilbites of brown,
But mainly the whites live in this town.
Finally, a word for some individuals not named.
They add variety to the group they have claimed.
To okenite, serandite, analcime, chabazite too,
Thanks to each and every one of you.
And now a parting word, to tell you all,
No matter the color or form - big or small -
Each individual and family alike
Has never quarreled or picked a fight.
We should take a lesson from these friends of mine.
Remember, it is not how brightly you shine,
But how you mix and how you blend.
That will determine if you made a friend.

1986

Organization

The pages that follow are organized into two major sections. The first contains photographs of what we'll call "The Main Collection." The second is dedicated to "The Cornwall Collection," minerals Milt collected on the job in the 1960s and early 70s. Following these two sections, an appendix includes several short pieces Milt wrote related to collecting, some of general interest and others about his own experience and collection, in particular. One of the articles in the appendix describes his ten-years of collecting microminerals, specimens so small they require a microscope to enjoy.

The photographs likely will be of most interest to readers. The photographs of The Main Collection are organized by chemical group, much as the actual display collection is. Each new section is introduced with a short explanation of what distinguishes that chemical group. The Cornwall Collection, however, is not organized by chemical group. These specimens are grouped together simply because they were found together.

Some pages include captions and bits of text that illuminate something of interest. Of course, you may or may not find these bits interesting yourself! Feel free to ignore the text and enjoy the photographs.

The Main Collection

1"

The size of each specimen can be estimated by comparing it to the height of the Styrofoam mount, which is about 1" tall. Based on this standard, the specimen above is about 2" high and 4" wide.

Elbaite with Lepidolite, Quartz and Albite
Minas Gerais, Brazil

Minerals: AMAZONITE & SMOKY QUARTZ
721
Location: Pikes Peak Area, Colorado

SILICATES

Silicates are the largest and most diverse family of minerals on Earth. They're all built from the same tiny building block: one silicon atom joined to four oxygen atoms, forming a tetrahedron. These tetrahedra can link in different ways — chains, sheets, or frameworks — creating everything from the **quartz** in beach sand to **feldspar** in granite, **mica** flakes, and colorful **tourmalines**. Because silicon and oxygen are so common in Earth's crust, silicates are everywhere. But what makes them especially beautiful is how tiny amounts of other elements can add color. A bit of iron in quartz turns it purple, creating **amethyst**. A different twist in the iron — sometimes with a little natural heating — gives **citrine** its golden yellow color. Small changes create big beauty.

Minerals: AMOZONITE, SMOKEY QUARTZ and ALBITE
564
Location: Crystal Peak Lake George, Colorado

Minerals: SMOKEY QUARTZ and AMOZONITE
512
Location: Florissant, Colorado

Minerals: AMAZONITE
521
Location: Crystal Peak Area, Florissant, Colorado

Minerals: QUARTZ xl with DOLOMITE
715
Location: Middleville, NY

This is interesting because the crystal formed inside a cavity of the host rock. It's hard to break open the rock and preserve the crystal. I had the good sense to buy this specimen when I saw it in Tucson. — MLL

Minerals: QUARTZ
264
Location: Middleville, New York

Minerals: ORTHOCLASE and SMOKEY QUARTZ
566
Location: Harris Park, Park Co., Colorado

Minerals: QUARTZ on ALBITE and ORTHOCLASE
142
Location: Conway, New Hampshire

Minerals: QUARTZ with HEMATITE
730 CHALCOPYRITE and DOLOMITE
Location: Daye Mine, Hubei Prov., China

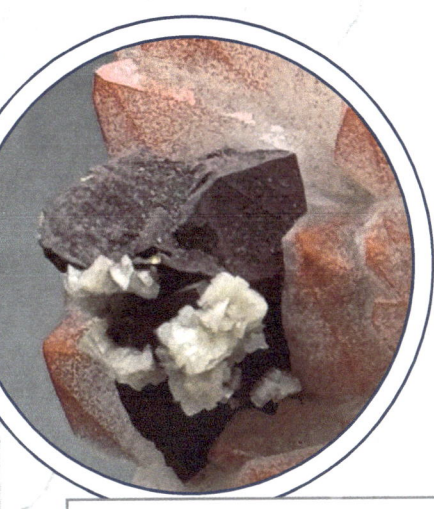

This specimen is especially appealing for the contrasting colors and different crystal structures that have formed on top of each other.

Minerals: ORTHOCLASE and QUARTZ
2
Location: Mina La Valenciana, Guanajuato, Mexico

Minerals: MORGANITE
618
Location: Nagar Mine, Gilgit, Packistan

Minerals: AMETHYST "flowers"
630
Location: Irai, Rio Grande do Sol, Brazil

Minerals: QUARTZ
668
Location: Santander, Columbia

Minerals: KUNZITE and ALBITE
617
Location: Nuristan, Afghanistan

Minerals: AQUAMARINE and
583   MUSCOVITE
Location: Upper Indus Valley, Nagar Mines
Gigit, Pakistan

Minerals: EMERALD
727
Location: Carnaiba Mine, Bahia, Brazil

Minerals: EMERALD in Biotite Schist
748
Location: Bahia, Brazil

Minerals: AMETHYST with HEMATITE inclusions
537
Location: Thunder Bay, Ontario

Mineral: CITRINE (heat treated?)
760
Location: Brazil ?

The One That Got Away

I was at the show in Tucson and a dealer had this emerald sitting on his table. I snapped the picture you see above and said I thought I'd be back for it. Less than an hour later, I returned and the emerald was gone. I couldn't believe he'd already sold it, and when I asked, the dealer couldn't even remember if he had sold it. It seemed just as likely that someone walked by the table and stuck it in his pocket. In any case, the emerald specimen was gone, and I've been sore about it ever since. — MLL

Minerals: QUARTZ
606
Location: Mt. Ida, Arkansas

A favorite of Milt's for the variety of crystal sizes and their unusual clarity.

Minerals: QUARTZ with HEMATITE
758
Location: Tarhbalt, Morocco

A favorite of Tim's for its rugged look and dramatic shadows.

Minerals: AMETHYST
707
Location: Uruguay

Minerals: QUARTZ with clay inclusions
719
Location: Minas Gerais, Brazil

Minerals: QUARTZ with HEMATITE
711
Location: Brazil

Minerals: DRAVITE on MUSCOVITE
347
Location: Yinnietharra, West Australia

Minerals: AMETHYST
603
Location: Uruguay

Minerals: ELBAITE and QUARTZ
427
Location: Brazil

Minerals: SCHORL on ORTHOCLASE
568
Location: Gilgit, Pakistan

Minerals: RUBELLITE on QUARTZ
508   with ALBITE
Location: Pala, California

Minerals: INDICOLITE on QUARTZ
709
Location: Mina Cruzeiro, Rento, Brazil

These specimens are all **tourmalines**. Tourmalines are a colorful and complex group of minerals known for their long, slender crystals and wide range of vibrant colors—including pink, green, blue, black, and even multicolored varieties, like "watermelon." The presence of different trace elements in the crystal accounts for the variety of colors.

Minerals: ELBAITE on MUSCOVITE
27   with QUARTZ
Location: Norway, Maine

Minerals RUBELLITE in QUARTZ
753:
Location: Arassuai, Minas Gerais, Brazil

Minerals: TOURMALINE "watermelon"
610   in QUARTZ with LEPIDOLITE
Location: Corouel Murta, Minas Gerais, Brazil

Minerals: KYANITE
723
Location: Cruzeiro Mine, Sao Jose da Safira, Minas Gerais, Brazil

I especially like this one because of its variety of crystal sizes and their different orientations. — MLL

Mineral: KYANITE
789
Location: Barra do Salinas, Coronel Murta, Minas Gerais, Brazil

Minerals: SCHORL with MUSCOVITE and HEMATITE matrix
787
Location: Minas Gerais, Brazil

Minerals: SCHORL with QUARTZ
662
Location: Minas Gerais, Brazil

Minerals: SPESSARTINE and SMOKEY QUARTZ with MUSCOVITE
675
Location: Fujian Province, China

Minerals: GROSSULAR
648
Location: Sierra de las Cruces "Lake Jaco Locality", Coahuila, Mexico

Minerals: GARNET on QUARTZ with ORTHOCLASE
631
Location: Dassu, above Shigar Baltistan, NA Pakistan

Minerals: HESSONITE
414
Location: Asbestos, Quebec

Minerals: PHLOGOPITE on CALCITE 698
Location: Namib Desert, Namibia

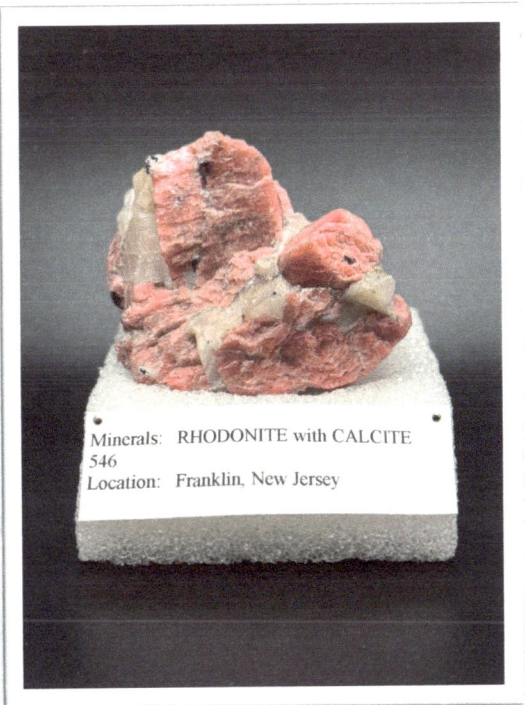

Minerals: RHODONITE with CALCITE 546
Location: Franklin, New Jersey

Minerals: MUSCOVITE on ALBITE 735
Location: Minas Gerais, Brazil

The muscovite crystals are "stacked plates" oriented the same way. It's the crystal alignment that's interesting. — MLL

Minerals: CLINOZOISITE and BYSSOLITE
6
Location: Cornog, Pa.

Minerals: AMETHYST
712
Location: Ayoreita, Bolivia

Minerals: HEMIMORPHITE
484
Location: Durango, Mexico

Minerals: ROSE QUARTZ crystals on
557   clear QUARTZ
Location: Taquaral, Minas Gerais, Brazil

Minerals: BRAZILIANITE in ALBITE
708
Location: Linopolis, Minas Gerais, Brazil

Minerals: DIOPTASE on CALCITE with
408   MALACHITE?
Location: Tsumeb, S.W. Africa

This was a special find! (1972) -- MLL

Mineral: "Green" OPAL
780
Location: Madagascar

Mineral: THULITE
785
Location: Leksvik, Norway

Labradorite looks like it's glowing from inside because of the way light interacts with thin layers in the stone. When light enters, it hits those layers and bounces around, creating a colorful flash as the rays overlap and reflect back. It's the same kind of effect you see in soap bubbles or peacock feathers—light getting split and scattered in beautiful ways. This shifting glow is called "**labradorescence**," and it's what makes labradorite look so magical.

Minerals: LAPIS LAZULI polished
697
Location: Sar-eSang Mine?
Jurm, Afghanistan

Mineral: LABRADORITE
790
Location: Ampanihy, Madagascar (est)

Minerals: CITRINE
650
Location: Minas Gerais, Brazil?

Minerals: CITRINE
549
Location: Minas Gerais, Brazil

Minerals: CITRINE and AMETHYST
746
Location: Magaliesberg
Pretoria, S Africa

Minerals: TOPAZ, QUARTZ, and
619 ORTHOCLASE
Location: Gilgit, Packistan

Minerals: TOPAZ on ALBITE with
589 ELBAITE
Location: Skardo, Gilgit, Pakistan

Minerals: HEMATITE with RUTILE in
573 QUARTZ
Location: Bahia, Brazil

Agate forms over millions of years when silica-rich water fills hollow spaces, usually in volcanic rock. As the water evaporates, silica builds up in colorful bands, creating the layered patterns we see today.

Minerals: LAGUNA LACE AGATE
751
Location: Chihuahua, Mexico

Minerals: CLINOCHLORE (seraphinite)
749
Location: Korshunoskiy Mine, Irkutskaya Oblast, Siberia, Russia

Minerals: BENITOITE and NEPTUNITE with NATROLITE
594
Location: Benitoite Gem Mine, California

ZEOLITES

Like quartz and tourmalines, zeolites are part of the silicate family. They form, however, in a more open, airy structure at the atomic level. Chemically, they're made of aluminum, silicon, and oxygen, with a framework that holds water and often includes calcium, sodium, or potassium. **Mesolite** (seen here) is a striking example, forming silky sprays of needle-like crystals. **Apophyllite**, often found with zeolites, grows in clear, blocky crystals that resemble glass. Their light, delicate structures and shared chemical pattern make zeolites especially popular among collectors for their beauty and variety.

Name: MESOLITE
Locality: POONA, INDIA
528

Minerals: HEULANDITE and STILBITE
611
Location: Jaljaon, India

Minerals: CHLORITE on HUELANDITE
624
Location: Poona, India

Minerals: MANGANOPECTOLITE on PREHNITE
293
Location: Lower New St. Quarry, Patterson, New Jersey

Minerals: MESOLITE
587
Location: Lonavla, India

Minerals: OKENITE on GYROLITE
497
Location: Bombay, India

Minerals: CAVANSITE on STILBITE
588
Location: Poona, India

Minerals: DATOLITE
676
Location: Central Boron Mine, Dal'Negorsk, Primorie, Russia

Minerals: PYROPHYLLITE
129
Location: Mariposa Co., California

Pyrophyllite and **Cavansite** often form in radiating clusters, where thin, flat crystals spread outward from a central point like spokes on a wheel or petals on a flower.

Minerals: APOPHYLLITE with HEULANDITE
531
Location: Poona, India

Minerals: APOPHYLLITE
612
Location: Jalgaon, India

Minerals: APOPHYLLITE on PREHNITE
275
Location: Fairfield Quarry, Centreville, Virginia

Minerals: PECTOLITE
221
Location: Lower New St. Quarry, Patterson, New Jersey

Minerals: SCOLECITE on HEULANDITE
737
Location: Aurangabad, India

Minerals: PHACOLITE
337
Location: Devonport, Tasmania

Mineral: CHALCEDONY
763
Location: Sulawesi, Indonesia

Minerals: THOMSONITE on
736　　　　　HEULANDITE
Location: Aurangabad, India

Minerals: CHALCEDONY variety
764　　CHRYSOPRASE with KAOLIN
Location: Indonesia

Minerals: ANALCIME, SERANDITE,
539 NATROLITE and POLYLITHIONITE
Location: Mont St. Hilaire, Quebec

Minerals: BABINGTONITE on
731 PREHNITE
Location: Qiaojia, Zhaotong Prefecture, Yunnan Province, China

Minerals: STELLERITE
579
Location: Grant Co., Oregon

Minerals: PREHNITE and CALCITE
464
Location: Prospect Park, New Jersey

Minerals: PREHNITE with THOMSONITE?
223
Location: Prospect Park, New Jersey

Minerals: STILBITE with NATROLITE
240 and PECTOLITE
Location: Prospect Park, New Jersey

I've always loved this one. — MLL

Minerals: STILBITE on QUARTZ
632
Location: Nasik, India

Minerals: HEULANDITE with STILBITE
633
Location: Jalgoan, India

Minerals: HEMATITE
590
Location: Newport Mine, Ironwood, Michigan

SULFIDES AND OXIDES

Sulfides and oxides aren't grouped together in official classification systems, but they often get talked about side by side because they share some practical and visual similarities. Both are made when a metal combines with just one other element — sulfur in the case of sulfides, and oxygen for oxides. Sulfides include minerals like **pyrite** (often called "fool's gold" for its metallic yellow crystals) and **galena** (a heavy lead ore with a silver-gray color and cubic form). Oxides include minerals like **hematite**, an iron-rich mineral that can look black and metallic or dusty and reddish, and **rutile**, a titanium oxide that often forms reddish-brown or golden needle-like crystals and is a major source of titanium. These minerals might not be as sparkly or colorful as some others, but they play a huge role in how we get metals that shape our everyday lives.

Minerals: HEMATITE
584
Location: Montreal Mine, Wisconsin

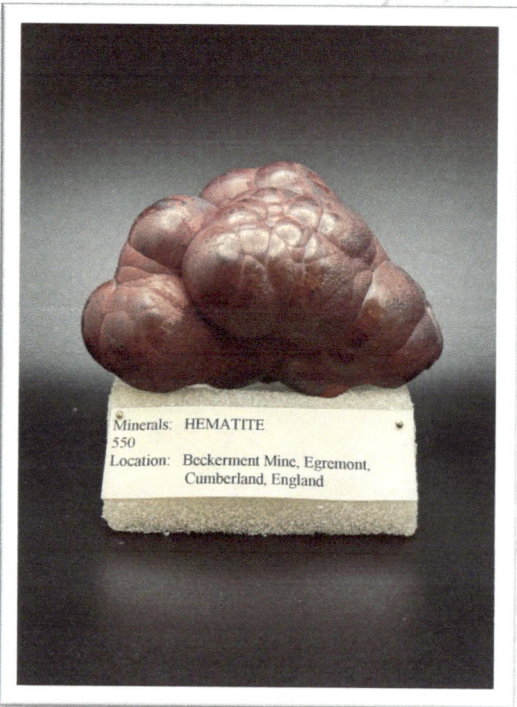

Minerals: HEMATITE
550
Location: Beckerment Mine, Egremont, Cumberland, England

Minerals: QUARTZ with HEMATITE
733
Location: Jinglong Mine, Guang Dong Province, China

Minerals: RUBY in MARBLE
755
Location: Chhumar Mines
Ganesh Himal, Nepal

Ruby is a red variety of **corundum**, a mineral made of aluminum and oxygen. Its red color comes from small amounts of chromium replacing aluminum in the crystal structure, which changes how light is absorbed. With different trace elements, the same mineral becomes a **sapphire** instead.

Minerals: GOETITE in CALCITE
147   coating CALCITE
Location: Santa Eulalia, Mexico

Minerals: RUTILE
567
Location: Graves Mountain
Lincoln Co., Georgia

Minerals: PSILOMELANE on WULFENITE
652   with CALCITE
Location: Glove Mine, Amado, Arizona

Mineral: MARCASITE var. cockscomb
42
Location: Joplin, Missouri

Minerals: PYRITE on Clay
593
Location: Navajun, Spain

Minerals: PYRITE
766
Location: Navajun, Spain

Minerals: SPHALERITE on PYRITE
767 on QUARTZ
Location: Huaron Mine, Huanzala, Peru

Minerals: PYRITE
765
Location: Huaron Mine, Huanzala, Peru

Minerals: SPHALERITE
429
Location: Joplin, Missouri

Minerals: SPHALERITE var. Marmatite
13
Location: Ouray, Colorado

Minerals: SPHALERITE, DOLOMITE, and PYRITE
41
Location: Naica, Durango, Mexico

Minerals: SPHALERITE and GALENA
559
Location: Peru

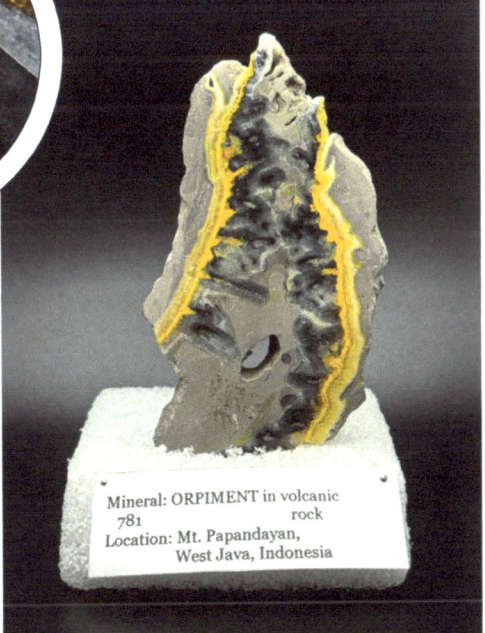

Mineral: ORPIMENT in volcanic rock
781
Location: Mt. Papandayan, West Java, Indonesia

Minerals: STIBNITE
491
Location: Bejutz, Romania

Minerals: GALENA
470
Location: 1000' Level, Sweetwater Mine, Bunker, Missouri

Mineral: GALENA
769
Location: Septemvri Mine, Rhodope Mts. Smolyan Oblast, Bulgaria

Galena is a shiny, silver-gray mineral known for its sharp, cubic crystals. It's a main source of lead, which is why it feels so heavy—lead is one of the densest common elements in the Earth's crust. Galena's clean lines, metallic luster, and solid weight make it a favorite among collectors, especially when the cubes are well-formed and neatly stacked.

Galena is so reflective that I had to angle this specimen away to photograph it. Otherwise, you'd see me and my camera in the reflection! — Tim

Minerals: GALENA with Dolomite and PYRITE
520
Location: Reynolds Co., Missouri

```
Minerals:  STIBNITE
687
Location:  Wuling Antimony Mine
           Jiangxi Prov., China
```

This specimen of **Stibnite** is actually two different pieces mounted together. When a friend who had never seen the collection visited, he zeroed in on this specimen quickly, saying, "This one has real Fortress of Solitude vibes." The Fortress of Solitude is Superman's hideaway and personal sanctuary, usually depicted as icy spears jutting up from the Arctic floor.   - Tim

Minerals: VANADINITE
509
Location: Mibladen, Morocco

PHOSPHATES AND OTHERS

Phosphates, tungstates, chromates, and molybdates may sound unrelated, but they're all built around the same basic shape: a central atom (like phosphorus, tungsten, chromium, or molybdenum) surrounded by four oxygen atoms, forming a tetrahedron. These groups, called oxyanions, bond with metals to form colorful and often striking crystals. For example, **vanadinite** is a bright red phosphate, **scheelite** is a glowing tungstate, and **wulfenite** is a deep orange chromate. They don't form large rock-forming families like silicates or carbonates, but they're prized by collectors and sometimes mined for their metals. They're a great example of how swapping out one central atom can lead to entirely new and distinct minerals — each with its own look and story.

Minerals: VANADINITE
671
Location: Morocco

Minerals: SCHEELITE on MUSCOVITE
714
Location: Si Chuang, China

Minerals: SCHEELITE with QUARTZ
684
Location: Xuebaoding Mt'n., Sichuan Prov., Pingwu Co., China

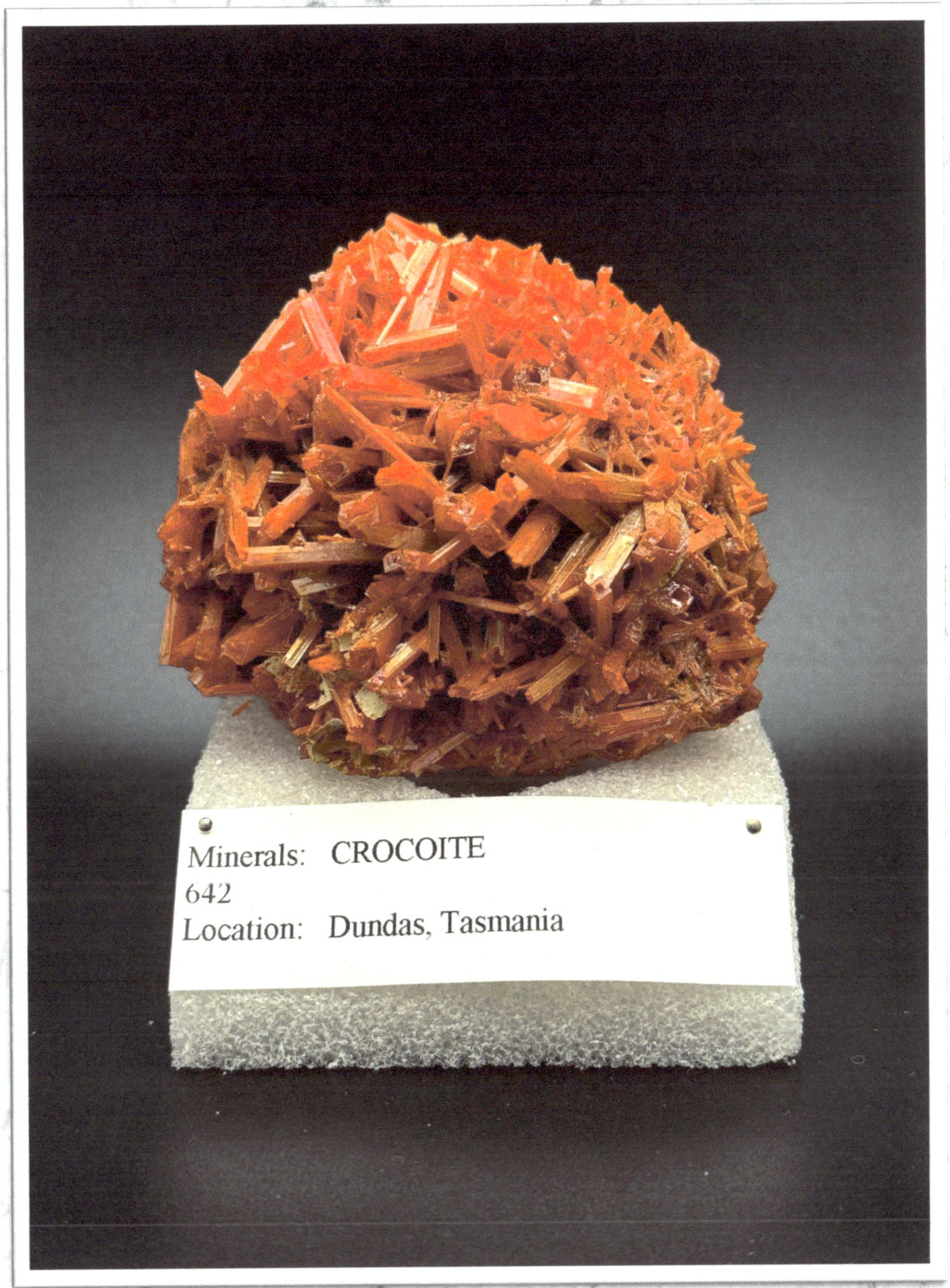
Minerals: CROCOITE
642
Location: Dundas, Tasmania

Minerals: CROCOITE
656
Location: Dundas, Tasmania

Minerals: WULFENITE on DOLOMITE
553
Location: Touissit, Oujda, Morocco

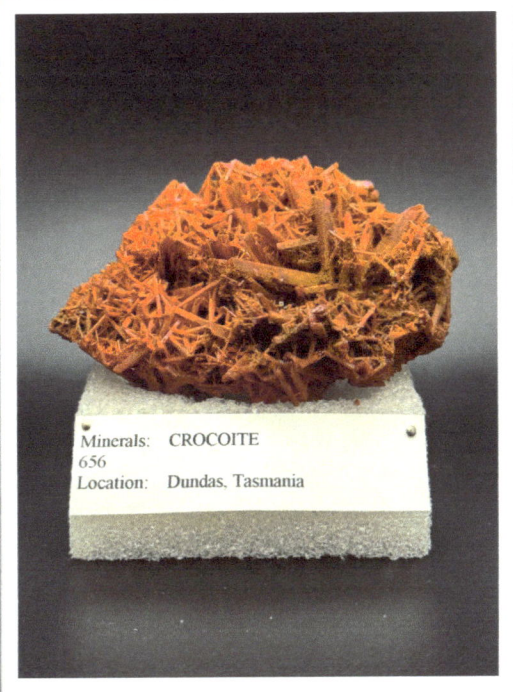

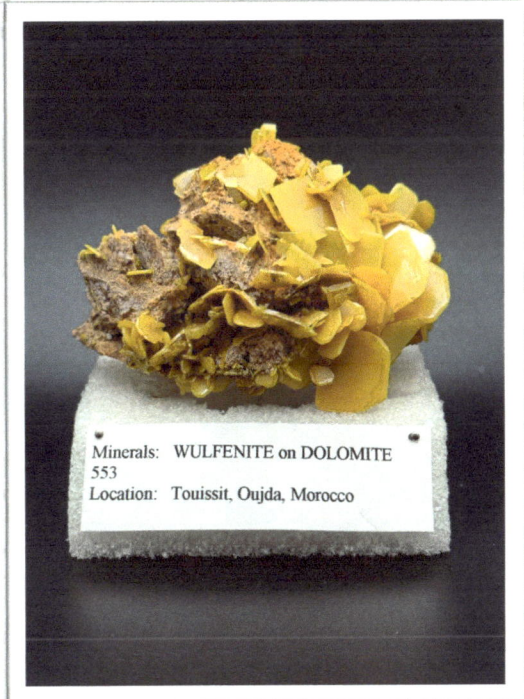

Minerals: WULFENITE
69
Location: Mexico

Minerals: WULFENITE and MIMETITE
523
Location: San Francisco Mine, Cerro Prieto, Sonora, Mexico

Minerals: VANADINITE on WULFENITE on OPAL
75
Location: Old Yuma Mine, Tucson, Ariz.

The blade-like orange crystals are wulfenite. You have to zoom in on those blades to see the microscopic vanadinite crystals.

Minerals: APATITE on CALCITE with AUGITE
538
Location: Yates Uranium Mine, Otter Lake, Quebec

Minerals: APATITE
682
Location: Cerro del Mercado Mine, Durango, Mexico

The beautiful color of the apatite crystal is hard to see against the host rock

Minerals: APATITE and CALCITE
591
Location: Baikal Lake, Sludanka, USSR

Minerals: PYROMORPHITE
658
Location: Daoping Mine, Yangshu, Guangxi Province, China

Mineral: PYROMORPHITE
778
Location: Daoping Mine, Yangshu, Guangxi Province, China

Minerals: WAVELITE
614
Location: Mt. Ida, Arkansas

Minerals: ADAMITE on LIMONITE
76
Location: Mapimi, Durango, Mexico

Minerals: ADAMITE
276
Location: Mapimi, Durango, Mexico

Minerals: ADAMITE and CALCITE on LIMONITE
149
Location: Mapimi, Mexico

Minerals: VARISCITE, WARDITE & CRANDALLITE
557
Location: Little Green Monster Mine
Fairfield, Utah

Minerals: TURQUOISE
694
Location: Tibet

Turquoise is loved for its vibrant blue to blue-green color, often with darker veins running through it. Instead of sharp crystals, it forms as smooth, rounded masses, easy to shape and polish. Its rich color and softness make it a favorite for jewelry makers, especially in rings, beads, and inlay work. For centuries, it's been prized for its beauty and calming, earthy tones.

Minerals: MIMETITE var. CAMPYLITE
392
Location: Red Gill Mine, Cumberland, England

Minerals: MIMETITE
51
Location: San Pedro Corralitos, Chihuahua, Mexico

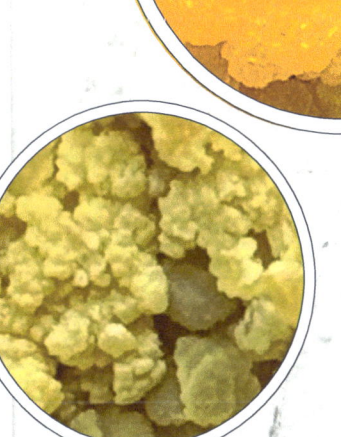

ELEMENTS

Native elements are the simplest kind of minerals — they're made of just one element. No combinations, no complicated formulas, just pure substances that crystallize on their own. Gold, silver, copper, and even diamonds (which are pure carbon) all belong to this group. Some native elements form shiny metallic crystals, while others, like sulfur, form bright-colored crystals instead. Even though they're simple, native elements can be spectacular. Gold can form beautiful leaf-like sheets, copper can grow into strange branching shapes, and diamonds need just the right conditions deep in the Earth to grow their famous crystals. These minerals are a good reminder that not all minerals are mixtures — sometimes a single element is enough.

The band of silver running through the copper may be difficult to see.

Minerals: GOLD in QUARTZ with FLUORITE
304
Location: Placer Co., California

Specimen 304

This beautiful gold specimen passed through many hands before becoming part of Milt Leet's collection in 1971.

The earliest record shows that a French mining engineer and noted collector of gold specimens named George De La Bouglise (1842-1911) owned this specimen. Upon his death, Parisian mineral dealer Alexandre Stuer held an auction, and Albert Burrage became its new owner. Burrage donated the specimen to Harvard University in 1948 and sometime in the next two decades, it came into the possession of collector Arthur Montgomery. Art was a professor at Lafayette College, and he used to take his classes to visit the Cornwall Iron Mine, where a young mining engineer named Milt Leet would lead them in a tour. In appreciation for all his help, Art gave this gold specimen to Milt in 1971, and it has been one of the highlights of the collection ever since.

As a kid, I remember classmates asking, "Does your dad have any gold?" For a kid, this is another way of asking if he has any Priceless Treasure. "Yes," I would say proudly and point to 304.

— Tim

Minerals: SULFUR with CELESTITE
608
Location: Machow Mine, Poland

Minerals: SULPHUR on ARAGONITE
540
Location: Girgenti, Sicily

Minerals: SULFUR on DOLOMITE
607
Location: Machow Mine, Poland

Minerals: SILVER (tarnished wires) on CALCITE
307
Location: Batopilas, Chihuahua, Mexico

As a child Julie thought Dad got this one wrong. "Silver isn't black!"

Mineral: SILICON
773
Location: Man Made

Mineral: SULFUR
772
Location: Maybee, Michigan

Minerals: CERUSSITE
542
Location: Flux Mine, Patagonia, Arizona

CARBONATES

Carbonates are a group of minerals built around the carbonate ion — one carbon atom bonded to three oxygen atoms (CO_3). This simple structure combines with metals like calcium, copper, or manganese to form a wide range of minerals. **Calcite** and **aragonite** are two of the most common; they share the same chemical formula ($CaCO_3$) but have different crystal structures. **Malachite**, with its deep green swirls, and **rhodochrosite**, famous for its rich pinks and reds, are also carbonates — their vivid colors come from trace metals like copper (in malachite) and manganese (in rhodochrosite). Even though many carbonates are soft and easily worn down, they often form beautifully patterned crystals, cave formations, and colorful mineral specimens.

Minerals: CERUSSITE and DUFTITE
10
Location: Tsumeb, SW Africa

Minerals: CERUSSITE
532
Location: Tsumeb, SW Africa

This specimen of reticulated **Cerussite** broke into two pieces when we moved the collection into my home. When remounting it, I thought this upright orientation showed off the specimen best. Later I realized Specimen 532 now resembled the "L" on the ring Champ May Leet wore every day of his adult life. Champ was Milt's father and my grandfather.   - Tim

Minerals: ARAGONITE
725
Location: Potosi Mine, Santa Eulalia Dist., Chihuahua, Mexico

Minerals: ARAGONITE
716
Location: Morocco

Mineral: ARAGONITE
761
Location: Morocco (or Sicily ?)

Minerals: ARAGONITE on SELENITE
485
Location: Cuenca, Spain

Minerals: ARAGONITE
729
Location: Morocco

Minerals: CALCITE with HEMATITE
626
Location: Santa Eulalia, Chihuahua, Mexico

Minerals: CALCITE in Limestone
629
Location: Elmwood Mine, Carthage, Tenn.

Minerals: CALCITE on FLUORITE
634
Location: Elmwood Mine, Carthage, Tenn.

Minerals: CALCITE on GALENA
487
Location: Sweetwater Mine, Reynolds Co., Missouri

Minerals: CALCITE on AMETHYST
732
Location: Rio Grande do Sul, Brazil

Minerals: CALCITE
696
**Location: Vulcan Mine
Racine, Wisconsin**

I looked long and hard for this specimen and was very pleased when I finally found it. Kyana Show in Plymouth, Wisconsin. — MLL

Minerals: GALENA and CALCITE
669
Location: Fletcher Mine, Reynolds Co. Missouri

Minerals: CALCITE and PYRITE
536
Location: Brushy Creek Mine, Reynolds Co., Missouri

Minerals: COPPER in CALCITE
575
Location: Keweenaw Point, Michigan

Minerals: DOLOMITE
450
Location: Binkley & Ober Quarry
East Petersburg, Pa

Minerals: CALCITE
605
Location: San Antonio Mine
Chihuahua, Mexico

Minerals: CALCITE on DOLOMITE
544
Location: Blackrock, Arkansas

inclusions

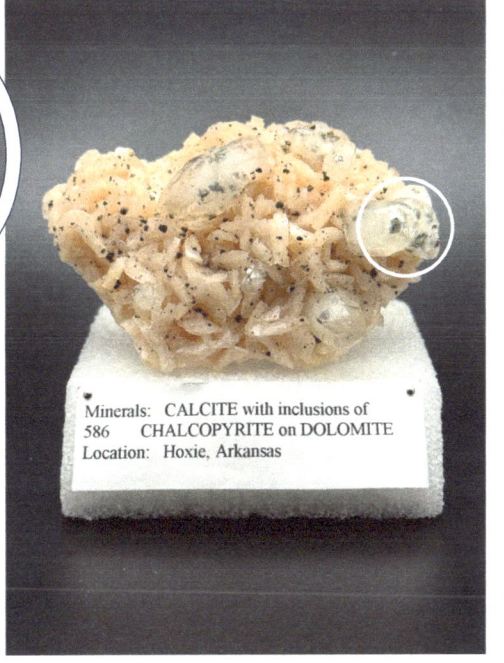

Minerals: CALCITE with inclusions of
586   CHALCOPYRITE on DOLOMITE
Location: Hoxie, Arkansas

Minerals: COBALTOCALCITE
592
Location: Zaire, Africa

Minerals: COBALTOCALCITE
759
Location: Bou Azzer, Morocco

Minerals: CALCITE
495
Location: Paul Frank Quarry,
North Vernon, Indiana

Mineral: CALCITE in clam shell
779
Location: Fort Drum Crystal Mine
Okeechobee Co., Florida

Minerals: CALCITE (septarian nodule)
673
Location: Orderville, Utah

Minerals: SEPTARIAN NODULE
752 (cut and polished)
Location: Orderville, Utah

It looks like a calcite crystal, but it's actually made of sand. The original calcite dissolved over time, and sand filled the empty space, keeping the crystal's shape. This "pseudomorph" is nature's version of a cast—a crystal-shaped memory made entirely of sand.

Minerals: CALCITE pseudomorph of Sand
452
Location: Rattlesnake Butte, Washington Co., South Dakota

I always thought this one looked like whales under water. – Julie

Minerals: CALCITE
535
Location: West Yellowstone, Montana

Minerals: CALCITE
462
Location: Meade Co., South Dakota

Minerals: RHODOCROSITE with CALCITE
570
Location: Capnic, Romania

Minerals: CALCITE
443
Location: Chihuahua, Mexico

Minerals: MANGANOCALCITE
702
Location: Daye Co., Hubei Prov., Huangshi Prefecture, China

Minerals: MANGANOCALCITE
355
Location: Lordsburg, New Mexico

Minerals: CALCITE (phantom) with PYRITE
625
Location: Brushy Creek Mine, Reynolds Co., Missouri

Minerals: CALCITE 574 Location: Santa Eulalia, Chihuahua, Mexico	 Minerals: CALCITE 112 Location: Mexico	 Minerals: AZURITE 643 Location: Arizona
 Minerals: MALACHITE on COBALTOAN DOLOMITE 604 Location: Kakanda, Katanga, Zaire	 Minerals: MALACHITE and AZURITE 756 Location: Liu Feng Shan Mine, Anhui Province, China	 Minerals: MALACHITE 693 Location: Mashamba Mine Dikulwe, Congo

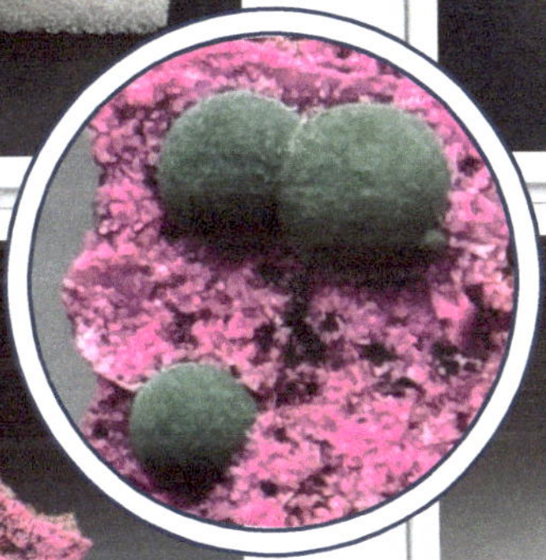

Mineral: AZURITE on siltstone
783
Location: Malbunka Mine, North Territory, Australia

Minerals: MALACHITE polished
654
Location: Zaire, Africa

Malachite and **azurite** look strikingly different—malachite is deep green, while azurite is bright blue—but they are closely related minerals. Both are copper carbonates that often form together when copper-rich water reacts with limestone or similar rocks. Their color difference comes from slight changes in atomic structure. Found side by side or even mixed in a single specimen, they are favorites among collectors and jewelers.

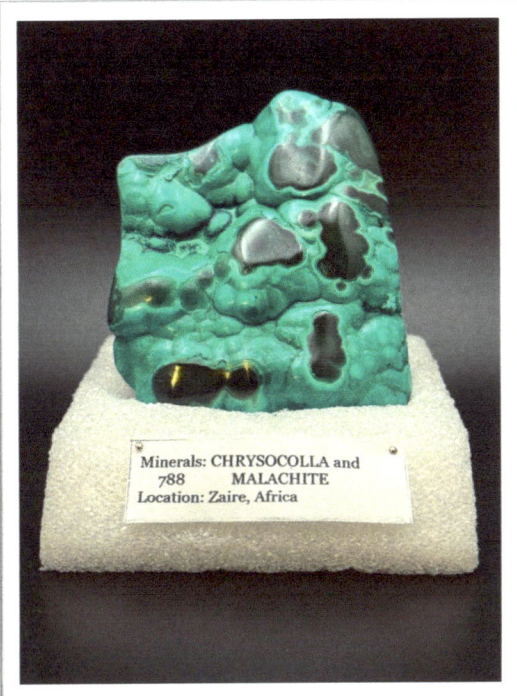

Minerals: CHRYSOCOLLA and MALACHITE
788
Location: Zaire, Africa

Minerals: MALACHITE on CALCITE
527
Location: Tsumeb, SW Africa

Minerals: CHRYSOCOLLA on MALACHITE
670
Location: Zaire, Africa

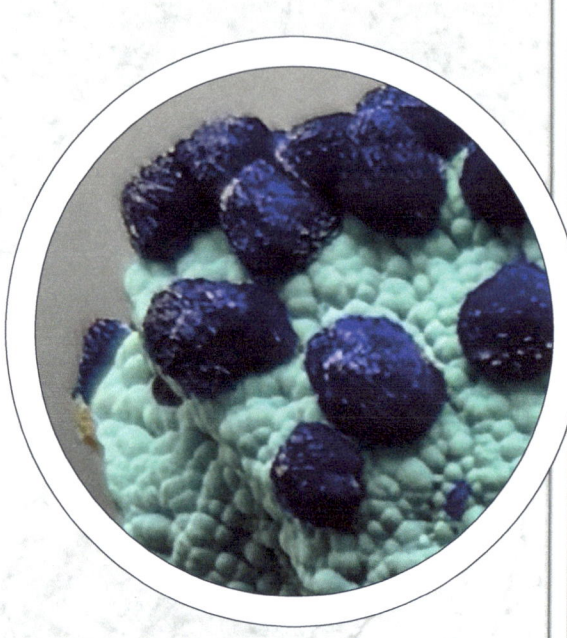

Minerals: AZURITE on MALACHITE
526
Location: Metcalf Mine, Morenci, Arizona

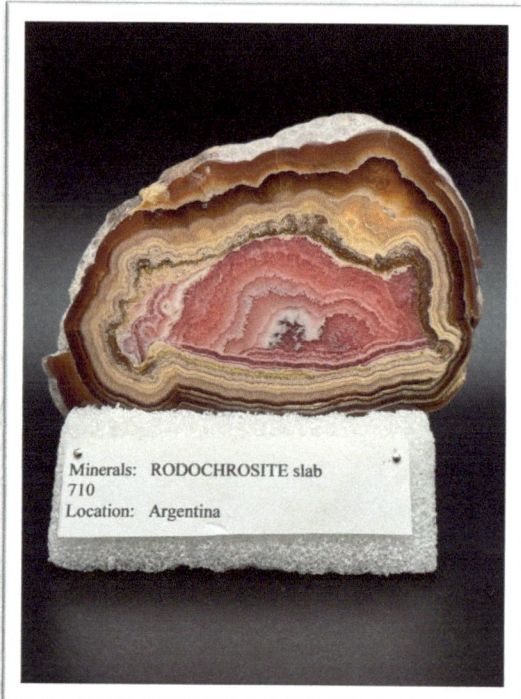

Minerals: RODOCHROSITE slab
710
Location: Argentina

Minerals: RHODOCHROSITE on QUARTZ
20
Location: Silverton, Colorado

Rhodochrosite can grow in stalactite-like shapes when slow drips of mineral-rich water leave behind thin layers over time. These layers build up and create pink and white bands. When the stalactite is cut open, you can see beautiful rings, a bit like tree rings or banded agate.

Minerals: RHODOCHROSITE
38
Location: Catamarca Prov., Argentina

Minerals: RHODOCHROSITE
601
Location: Museum Pocket, Tetrahedrite Stope, Sweet Home Mine, Alma, Colorado

Minerals: BORAX altering to TINCALCONITE
515
Location: West Jennifer Mine, Boron, California

Smithsonite often forms smooth, rounded shapes that look like bubbles or grape clusters. Instead of sharp edges, it grows in gentle layers, giving it a soft, polished appearance - more like melted wax than a typical crystal.

Minerals: SMITHSONITE
296
Location: Kelly Mine, Magdalena, N.M.

Minerals: SMITHSONITE and CALCITE
689
Location: Unknown

Minerals: SMITHSONITE
349
Location: Choix, Sinaloa, Mexico

HALIDE - FLUORITES

Halides are a major group of minerals formed when a metal bonds with a halogen element such as fluorine, chlorine, or iodine. One of the most well-known halides is **Fluorite**, famous for its wide-range of colors. Fluorite commonly forms perfect cubic shapes and is known for its ability to fluoresce under ultraviolet light, adding to its appeal. In contrast, **Halite --** also a halide -- consists of sodium and chlorine, making it essentially rock salt. Halite typically forms translucent, cubic crystals and is chemically different from fluorite because it contains chloride ions instead of fluoride. These minerals add a wide range of colors and crystal shapes that bring variety to the collection.

Minerals: HALITE
569
Location: Poland

Minerals: FLUORITE
502
Location: Coahuilla, Mexico

Minerals: FLUORITE on Limestone
635
Location: Elmwood Mine, Carthage, Tenn.

Minerals: FLUORITE
636
Location: Elmwood Mine, Carthage, Tenn.

Minerals: FLUORITE ball on QUARTZ
706
Location: Ajanta near Aurangabad, India

Fluorite, sunny-side up

Minerals: FLUORITE with phantom xl.
377
Location: Minerva Mine, Cave In Rock, Ill.

The environmental conditions during which the yellow fluorite crystal developed changed, resulting in its inclusion in the larger blue fluorite crystal. Notice the sharp transition line and that the juncture of the yellow and blue fluorite appears purple.

Minerals: FLUORITE
647
Location: Mina Navidad near Abasolo, Durango, Mexico

This is one of the more intense green fluorites you'll find. The greenest of the green. I waited a long time to buy this one! - MLL

Minerals: FLUORITE
646
Location: Wise Mine, Westmoreland, New Hampshire

Minerals: FLUORITE
273
Location: Blanchard Mine, Bingham, New Mexico

Minerals: FLUORITE & CELESTITE
685
Location: White Rock Quarry Clay Center, Ohio

Minerals: CELESTITE & FLUORITE
776
Location: Stoneco Quarry Clay Center, Ohio

Minerals: FLUORITE and CALCITE
639
Location: Minerva #1 Mine, Hardin Co., Illinois

Minerals: FLUORITE
580
Location: Denton Mine Cave In Rock, Illinois

Minerals: FLUORITE on QUARTZ 768
Location: Berbes, Spain

Minerals: FLUORITE and CALCITE 94
Location: Cave In Rock, Illinois

Fluorite comes in many colors, even though its chemical formula doesn't change. That's because tiny differences in how it forms—like traces of other elements or natural radiation—can change how it reflects light. These small changes don't alter the formula (CaF_2) but they do create a wide range of beautiful colors, from purple and blue to green, yellow, pink, brown, and even black.

Minerals: FLUORITE and CALCITE 496
Location: Cave In Rock, Illinois

Minerals: FLUORITE 713
Location: Jiangxi, Xinjiang, China

Mineral: FLUORITE 784
Location: Hardin Co., Illinois

Minerals: FLUORITE
645
Location: Xianghualin, Hunan Prov., China

Minerals: FLUORITE on CALCITE
375
Location: Gaskin Mine, Pope Co., Illinois

Minerals: FLUORITE
703
Location: Rogerley Mine, Weardale Dist., England

Minerals: FLUORITE
695
Location: Cave In Rock, Illinois

Minerals: FLUORITE
494
Location: Fort Wayne, Indiana

Minerals: FLUORITE with PYRITE
754
Location: Cave-in-Rock District Southern Illinois

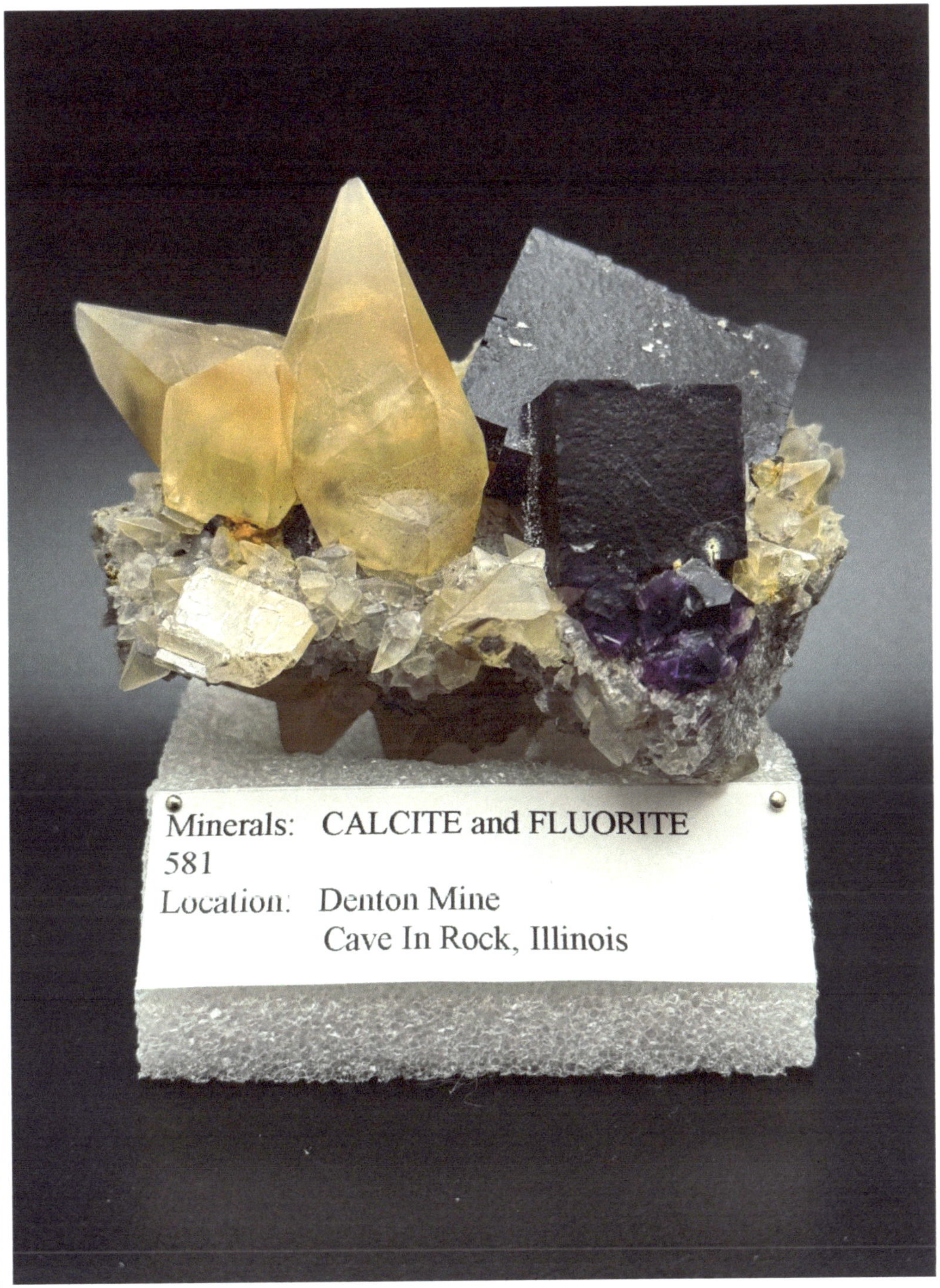

Minerals: CALCITE and FLUORITE
581
Location: Denton Mine
Cave In Rock, Illinois

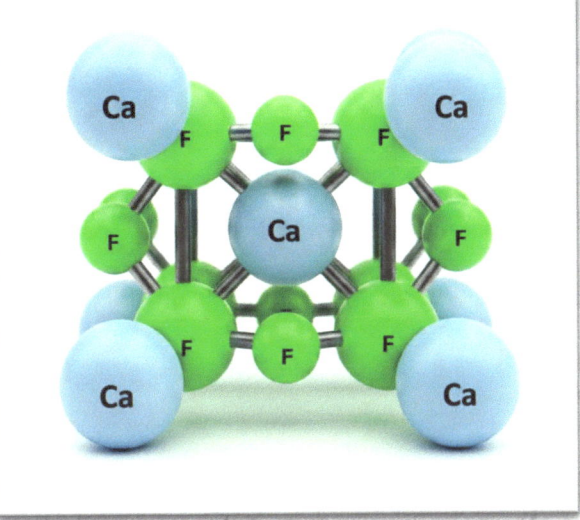

Fluorite has a cubic crystal structure, which is one of the simplest and most symmetrical in mineralogy. Each calcium ion (Ca^{2+}) is surrounded by eight fluoride ions (F^-), and each fluoride ion is surrounded by four calcium ions. This forms a repeating, tightly packed grid—like a 3D checkerboard—called the isometric system.

Minerals: CALCITE with CELESTITE and SULFUR
659
Location: Maybee, Michigan

SULFATES

Sulfates are minerals formed when a metal combines with the sulfate group — one sulfur atom bonded to four oxygen atoms (SO_4). They often form in places where water evaporates and usually develop light-colored, well-shaped crystals. **Barite** contains barium and is known for its unusually high density, making it one of the heaviest common minerals. **Selenite** is a clear, delicate form of gypsum made of calcium sulfate with water molecules in its structure. **Celestite** contains strontium and is prized for its pale blue crystals, often found in geodes or sedimentary rocks, where its gentle color contrasts beautifully with surrounding minerals. Although all three share the sulfate group, the different metal elements — barium, calcium, and strontium — give each mineral distinct properties and appearances.

This specimen is typical of the thing that first attracted me to displaying a variety of color in my collection. This is the sort of thing I went for first. — MLL

Minerals: CELESTITE with STRONTIANITE
45
Location: Gibbonburg, Ohio

Minerals: SELENITE
492
Location: Swan Hill, Victoria, Australia

Minerals: SELENITE
213
Location: Chihuahua, Mexico

Minerals: CELESTITE on CALCITE
66
Location: Lime City, Ohio

Minerals: SELENITE
640
Location: Senora Desert, Mexico

Minerals: SELENITE on QUARTZ on rock base
734
Location: Curvelo, Minas Gerais, Brazil

Minerals: SELENITE
489
Location: Villa Ahumada, Chihuahua, Mexico

Minerals: SELENITE
620
Location: Pernatys Lagoon, South Australia

Mineral dealers found when they whitened the edges of selenite specimens with a blowtorch, they sold a lot more specimens! This look isn't natural. — MLL

Minerals: SELENITE
678
Location: Las Salinas, Otume, Peru

Minerals: SELENITE
677
Location: Las Salinas, Otume, Peru

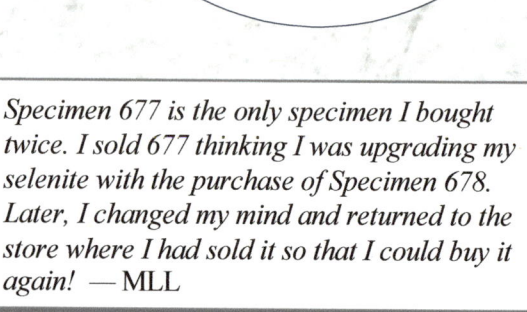

Specimen 677 is the only specimen I bought twice. I sold 677 thinking I was upgrading my selenite with the purchase of Specimen 678. Later, I changed my mind and returned to the store where I had sold it so that I could buy it again! — MLL

Minerals: SELENITE
534
Location: Swan Hill, Victoria, Australia

Minerals: SELENITE var. ram's horn
241
Location: Mexico

Minerals: CHALCOPYRITE on BARITE
328
Location: Saverland, Dreislar, Germany

Minerals: BARITE and CERUSSITE
529
Location: Mibladen, Morocco

Minerals: BARITE
348
Location: Gilman, Colorado

Minerals: BARITE
558
Location: Rock River, Yukon Territory

Minerals: BARITE on drusy QUARTZ
26
Location: Jefferson Co., Missouri

This was an early specimen in my collection. I used to see this sort of thing in the fields I'd collect in when I was a kid living in Missouri. — MLL

Minerals: BARITE on CALCITE
577
Location: Stoneham, Weld Co., Colorado

Mineral: BARITE
782
Location: Linwood Mine, Buffalo, Iowa

Minerals: BARITE with MALACHITE 743
Location: Mashamba West Mine
Katanga Province
Democratic Republic, Congo

Minerals: CREEDITE 700
Location: Mina Navidad, Abasolo
Durango, Mexico

Minerals: BARITE on CALCITE 473
Location: Elk Creek, South Dakota

I chased this one for a long time before I finally thought I could afford it. Beautiful crystals! — MLL

THE CORNWALL COLLECTION

CORNWALL IRON MINE

Located in Lebanon County, Pennsylvania, the Cornwall Iron Mine—also known as the Cornwall Ore Banks—was among the most enduring iron-ore operations in North America, running continuously from around 1739 until its closure in 1973. Founded by Peter Grubb in the late 1730s after discovering rich magnetite deposits, the mine supplied raw ore to the Cornwall Iron Furnace, which began smelting in 1742. The furnace was operated during the American Revolution by Grubb's sons; Curtis and Peter Jr. produced cannon and shot for George Washington's army.

After passing to Robert Coleman in the late 1790s, the operation grew into Pennsylvania's first million-dollar iron enterprise. Under Coleman's leadership and later Bethlehem Steel's control (after 1926), output surged—reaching over half a million tons annually by the 1890s. Techniques evolved from benches and trenches to large open pits and underground shafts, supported by railways and steam-powered hoisting.

Despite continued production after the furnace's 1883 shutdown, escalating costs, ore depletion, repeated flooding (most notably from Tropical Storm Agnes in 1972), and competition from richer western deposits led Bethlehem Steel to cease mining in June 1973. By then, the mines had produced over 106 million tons of iron ore.

Today, the Cornwall Iron Furnace site is a National Historic Landmark museum showcasing 18th- and 19th-century blast-furnace technology. The nearby flooded open-pit mine has become a scenic lake, visible from public hiking trails—a poignant reminder of an industrial landscape shaped over more than two centuries.

The "miners" in the photograph on the left look like they are on a rollercoaster. Actually, they are on-board the conveyance system that took workers at Cornwall underground each day. Milt is standing to the right of the skip. The year is 1968, and he is leading a tour of students from Delaware University, something he enjoyed and did often. Milt is with some coworkers in the photograph above.

The photograph in the upper-left corner is another tour group. This group came from the Bloomsburg State Teachers College. The year was 1970.

The other two pictures were staged by a photographer for reasons Milt never learned! To the left, he is standing in front of one of the ventilation fans that kept clean air moving through the mine. Above, he is inspecting the collapsable steel form used to support concrete above the drift (i.e., the tunnel).

Collecting at Cornwall

This short piece was written in 2000, but it recounts Milt's experience collecting minerals at Cornwall decades earlier.

In the early 1970's, periodic visits were made to an abandoned area of Number 3 Mine. There were at that time two ways to reach an area in the footwall of the mine where the faulted diabase had allowed evolving gases and solutions to form occurrences of natrolite, laumontite, apophyllite and analcite. One could descend from the pit on a 300-foot ladder into the pump room at the end of number 56 slushing drift, or go down the No. 3 shaft at the west end of the pit and walk back to the east on 6th level to 56 slushing drift. Either way, a collector after 6 hours could expect to recover about ten 1.5x1.5-inch specimens and three or four 2x3 inch specimens.

As I walked into the old pump room, which still had steel sets supporting the 20-foot-high roof, the smell of rotting timber gave a musty odor to the cool, damp, dark surroundings. Most cavities had been first exposed in the early 50s and specimens were taken at that time and preserved in the Leighton Donely collection at Cornwall. Some cavities were as large as two feet wide, but only high enough to allow for the passage of a hand and forearm. It was possible to extend a hand beyond an elbow in some cavities. At times ice cold water was encountered and only short durations of exposure could be endured. At other times needles of natrolite would penetrate the skin and had to be removed later with a knife. In addition to the pump room, several finger openings in the slushing drift near the pump room offered additional collecting. These openings were never developed, but the openings did allow access to the diabase from the concrete lined drift.

It was rare that only one mineral was found alone. Usually, apophyllite and analcite were found together; and occasionally natrolite and laumontite would partially cover the other two minerals. Apophyllite was found in a rosette growth pattern. Some rosettes were green from chlorite inclusions and had pink cores. Most were clear in color and reached as large as 1.5 inches in diameter. Needles of natrolite no thicker than a pencil lead reached lengths of four inches. Analcite crystals were found to a size of one inch. The laumontite crystals were very small microcrystals.

Collecting these specimens has been a joy. Feeling deep into a cavity and finding a smooth crystal face and knowing when it was exposed it would be beautiful, gave me a special time of excitement. What a contrast to be in such a drab, musty darkness and shine a light on a beautiful work of nature. I will never forget the experience.

Mineral: NATROLITE
7
Location: No. 3 Mine, Cornwall, Pa.

The Leet family moved from Pennsylvania to Ohio in 1978. Legend has it that Milt asked Gerry to hold this fragile piece of natrolite on her lap during the entire 8-hour drive. Now that's love (Gerry for Milt...Milt for the natrolite).

Minerals: LAUMONTITE on ANALCIME with APOPHYLLITE and NATROLITE on Diabase
280
Location: No.3 Mine, Cornwall, Pa.

Can you spot the white poodle? It's a bit like seeing shapes in the clouds. – MLL

Minerals: STILBITE
388
Location: 1140 SE Haulage Drift No.4 Mine, Cornwall, Pa.

Minerals: MAGNETITE
663
Location: Grace Mine, Morgantown, Pa.

The white antigorite had to be scraped away with a blade to reveal the black magnetite crystals beneath.

Minerals: APOPHYLLITE rosettes
237
Location: No.3 Mine, Cornwall, Pa.

Minerals: PYRITE iridescent on STILBITE
367
Location: No.4 Mine, Cornwall, Pa.

Minerals: APOPHYLLITE with ANALCIME
163 covered with NATROLITE
Location: No.3 Mine, Cornwall, Pa.

Minerals: MAGNETITE
454
Location: 201 Slushing Drift, Grace Mine
Morgantown, Penna.

The largest of these beautiful magnetite crystals are about an inch across. Magnetite is the strongest naturally occurring magnetic mineral on earth.

Minerals: NATROLITE
287   on Diabase
Location: No.3 Mine
Cornwall, Pa.

Minerals: STILBITE
369
Location: No.4 Mine, Cornwall, Pa.

Mineral: NATROLITE balls on Diabase
19
Location: No. 4 Mine, Cornwall, Pa.

Natrolite crystals may form balls like this specimen or slender needles like Specimen 12 on this page or fine hairs like Specimen 8 on the next page.

Mineral: NATROLITE
12
Location: No. 3 Mine Cornwall, Pa.

Minerals: ANALCIME with
325 APOPHYLLITE rosettes
Location: No.3 Mine, Cornwall, Pa.

Minerals: MAGNETITE in Talc
664
Location: Grace Mine, Morgantown, Pa.

Minerals: CHALCOPYRITE
188
Location: East End Ore Body Pit
No.3 Mine, Cornwall, Pa.

Mineral: STILBITE
22
Location: No. 4 Mine, Cornwall, Pa.

Minerals: PYRITE iridescent with
291   STILBITE on Blue Conglomerate
Location: No.4 Mine, Cornwall, Pa.

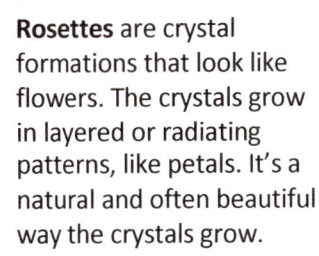

Rosettes are crystal formations that look like flowers. The crystals grow in layered or radiating patterns, like petals. It's a natural and often beautiful way the crystals grow.

Minerals: NATROLITE spray, rosettes of
8   APOPHYLLITE and ANALCIME
Location: No. 3 Mine, Cornwall, Pa.

Minerals: MAGNETITE in Talc
447
Location: Grace Mine, Morgantown, Pa.

The label on Specimen 447 as well as several other magnetite specimens say that the crystals are in Talc. It was later determined that the host material is actually Antigorite, which is a variety of Serpentine (seen on page 88).

Minerals: PYRITE on STILBITE
370
Location: No.4 Mine, Cornwall, Pa.

Minerals: NATROLITE
247
Location: No.3 Mine, Cornwall, Pa.

Minerals: APOPHYLLITE and ANALCIME
365 with NATROLITE on Diabase
Location: No.3 Mine, Cornwall, Pa.

Minerals: STILBITE with CALCITE
418
Location: No.4 Mine, Cornwall, Pa.

Minerals: MAGNETITE in Talc
448
Location: Grace Mine, Morgantown, Pa.

Mineral: STILBITE on Diabase
49
Location: No. 4 Mine, Cornwall, Pa.

Minerals: MAGNETITE
78
Location: No.4 Mine, Cornwall, Pa.

Minerals: PYRITE on STILBITE on Diabase
4
Location: No. 4 Mine, Cornwall, Pa.

Specimens 4 and 119 both show "transition zones." The chemical or physical environment that allowed the pyrite to form on the underlying stilbite changed from one side of the zone to the other.

Minerals: PYRITE on STILBITE
119
Location: No. 4 Mine, Cornwall, Pa.

Minerals: Serpentine with Limestone
364
Location: East End Ore Body, Cornwall, Pa.

Minerals: MAGNETITE
666
Location: No. 3 Mine, Cornwall, Pa.

Minerals: NATROLITE
62
Location: No. 4 Mine, Cornwall, Pa.

Serpentine is a smooth, often green rock found in places with a lot of historic tectonic activity, like California, Pennsylvania, China, and Italy. Specimen 364 was collected at Cornwall, but the frog was carved from serpentine in China. Displayed together in the collection, they are a reminder of the deep connection shared even by far-flung locations around the globe.

Minerals: ANALCIME, APOPHYLLITE, NATROLITE and LAUMONTITE
64
Location: No. 3 Mine, Cornwall, Pa.

Some **pyrite** appears rainbow-colored because of a thin surface layer that forms when it's exposed to air or moisture. This layer bends light, like a soap bubble or oil slick, creating iridescent colors.

Minerals: PYRITE iridescent on STILBITE
47
Location: No.4 Mine, Cornwall, Pa.

Minerals: CALCITE on STILBITE
665
Location: No.4 Mine, Cornwall, Pa.

Minerals: NATROLITE on ANALCIME
363 with Diabase
Location: No.3 Mine, Cornwall, Pa.

Minerals: PYRITE on STILBITE
1
Location: No. 4 Mine, Cornwall, Pa.

This is Specimen 1. Expecting a story, I asked Dad why this pyrite specimen from Cornwall had the distinction of being first. "I guess that's just the first one I picked up when I renumbered them all." Imagine my disappointment.
— Tim

Minerals: LAUMONTITE on NATROLITE
362   on ANALCIME on APOPHYLLITE
Location: No.3 Mine, Cornwall, Pa.

Minerals: MAGNETITE
750
Location: No. 4 Mine, Cornwall, Pa.

Minerals: APOPHYLLITE rosettes on
194   ANALCIME
Location: No.3 Mine, Cornwall, Pa.

Minerals: APOPHYLLITE rosettes on Diabase
361
Location: No.3 Mine, Cornwall, Pa.

Minerals: CALCITE on STILBITE
371
Location: No.4 Mine, Cornwall, Pa.

Milt gathered specimens from Cornwall and assembled the display you see above for a showing at the 1971 Earth Science and Gem Show. It was a promotional and public relations gesture by the management of Bethlehem Steel, but for Milt, it was nothing but fun.

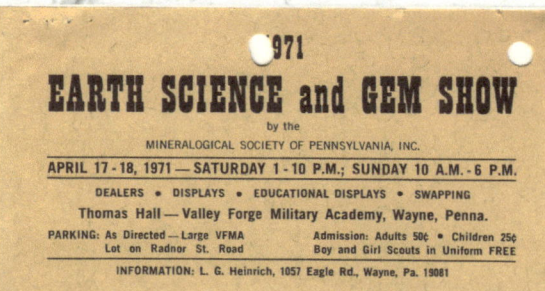

March 11, 1971

TO: H. Olsen

Concerning the attached letter from the Mineralogical Society of Pennsylvania, I think this would be a wonderful chance for Cornwall to show a complete suite of Cornwall rocks and minerals. It would be an excellent piece of inexpensive public relations work to do this. In fact I have talked to M. Leet, and as you know, he is extremely interested in minerals and he would be happy to accompany the suite of minerals and put it together. I believe also that this would be an excellent short article for the Bethlehem Review, indicating Bethlehem Steel Company's willingness to promote educational displays for these type of affairs; certainly this is much better promotional material then many that the Company has shown in the past in the Bethlehem Review. In addition it is very inexpensive, practicaly no cost.

I heartedly recommend that we allow our minerals to be shown at this time at the Mineralogical Society of Pennsylvania show, the publicity for the company will be excellent.

Please advice:

M. LIPENSKY
General Superintendent

In fact I would go up for 1 day to look it over, with my son!

THE GOLDEN ROOM

On an ordinary day in 1964, I came to work at the Cornwall Number 4 Mine and was told to get my camera and go see what the workers had discovered overnight. They were forming a drift over fingers in order to undercut the iron ore. In the course of their work, they broke through a fault in the blue conglomerate rock. When they did, they exposed a large void in the rock formation. When I arrived that morning and shined my light into the void, the walls and ceiling lit up with sparkling golden light.

The floor, ceiling, and walls of this "Golden Room" were covered with pyrite on stilbite. The room was large enough for me to enter, maybe 12-feet high, 15-feet wide, and 20-feet long. This was no small pocket but something more like a chamber that nature had created in the rock. Enormous forces along fault lines in the blue conglomerate rock opened up this chamber, and over countless years in the presence of specific gasses and a just-right combination of heat and pressure, the golden pyrite formed on the stilbite. For a mineral collector working underground in the dirt and dim light, this discovery was a once-in-a-lifetime wonder, a discovery other collectors could only dream of.

I collected many specimens from the golden room. Several of them have remained in my display collection over the 60 years since our discovery. Photos of those specimens appear on pages 86, 87, and 90.

Minerals: PYRITE on STILBITE 119
Location: No. 4 Mine, Cornwall, Pa.

It makes a person wonder about all the other beautiful mysteries below ground waiting to be discovered. Nature is patient and doesn't seem to care if her beauty is ever discovered or appreciated by human beings. The day we discovered the Golden Room and the days that immediately followed were magical. I'll never forget the feeling.

CORNWALL APPENDIX

On page 4, I describe the collecting I did in an area of #3 Mine at Cornwall. This photograph shows me at that location breaking up boulders in a raise opening opposite the pumproom in 56 slushing drift. This location provided beautiful specimens of natrolite, apophyllite, and analcite that allowed me to grow my own collection by trading with others. — MLL

92149

INTER-OFFICE CORRESPONDENCE

BETHLEHEM STEEL

BETHLEHEM MINES CORPORATION - ORE
CORNWALL, PA.   March 4, 1971
                           FILE REF.

FROM   Milton L. Leet, Mining Engineer.

TO   M. Lipensky, General Superintendent.

SUBJECT   Cornwall Ore Deposits

    Last year about this time you had asked me to try to make some sections from No. 3 to No. 4 Mine, thinking perhaps we would find a connection between these ore bodies. From time to time I have tried to find the answer, but I've had problems interpreting between drill holes in areas between No. 3 and No. 4 because there has been so little drilling.

    Last Thursday I received from Davis Lapham, Chief Mineralogist, for our State Bureau of Topographic and Geologic Survey, a letter in answer to some questions I had asked. Mr. Lapham, is in my opinion, the best versed individual concerning our ore deposit at Cornwall. Below is the last paragraph, quoted from his letter. The roll which he speaks of is now called "Big Hill" and its in this area where No. 3 and No. 4 ore bodies were connected.

    "Enclosed are two preliminary map copies of structure at Cornwall from my comprehensive report that is now in the hands of our editor. A few small errors are present, but the maps may help you in drawing your cross sections. These were compiled by Carlyle Gray from Bethlehem Steel Corp. data. Detailed cross sections of the host limestone, the Mill Hill Slate, and the Blue Conglomerate cannot be drawn from one mine to the other because of erosion and because individual beds, or laminae, are not continuous: numerous small thrust slices are present. The chief reason why the two ore bodies are not continuous is that the diabase in between rolls upward and erosion has stripped off both ore and hornfels. Vertical displacement on the fault is a minor factor as you can see from Plate 22 (enclosed). In my report in press I believe I have proved that ore solutions moved from the No. 4 mine up and over the diabase westward into the No. 3 mine area. Sam Sims has read a preliminary copy of my report and you may wish to discuss your cross-section problems with him."

                                                                     Milton L. Leet
                                                                    Mining Engineer

MLL: wcf

This article (written around 1970) describes collecting magnetite crystals at Grace Mine.

MAGNETITE CRYSTALS AT GRACE MINE

Several years ago, I received a few pieces of magnetite crystals from the Grace Mine at Morgantown, Pennsylvania. After discussing the occurrence with several people, it was learned that the location might still be accessible. On February first, the writer, accompanied by others of the engineering staff, went to twenty production panel on second level. To my surprise, the area was accessible at some risk. Collecting sites were along the ribs of 200 and 201 slushing drifts and at one station cutout further north. Danger exists because of slabs of ore which have spalled away from the ribs and stand precariously. One is tempted to pick at these, but results could be fatal.

In each drift a section about twenty feet long (see Figure 1) has been partially replaced by magnetite with small veins of calcite, talc, chlorite, and an altered mineral which resembles clay and may have been tremolite originally. Recrystallized limestone comprises most host rock. Conditions for best crystal development were in talc located along the ore-limestone contact and into the ore zone about two to three feet.

Talc seams about one inch thick contain rhombic dodecahedrons (see Figure 2) from one-quarter to one inch in size. Recovering crystals is simple in talc, but getting a good crystal on matrix is difficult because the base to which these large crystals are attached is massive or poorly crystallized magnetite which breaks as easily as the large crystals.

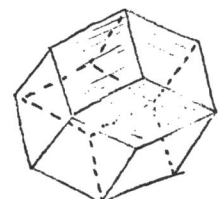

Fig. 2 - Magnetite Crystal from Grace Mine

Rhombic dodecahedron

The best specimens to date have come from a small area of alternating bands of talc and magnetite, each about two inches thick. It was best to remove prospective seams and after soaking in water a short time, pick away talc very carefully to expose the black crystals - which contrast nicely with remaining white talc.

The nicest, single crystal found is golf ball size and has three complete faces with six adjoining faces each half developed. Large size and sharp forms of rhombic dodecahedrons make these magnetite crystals unique.

— Milt Leet

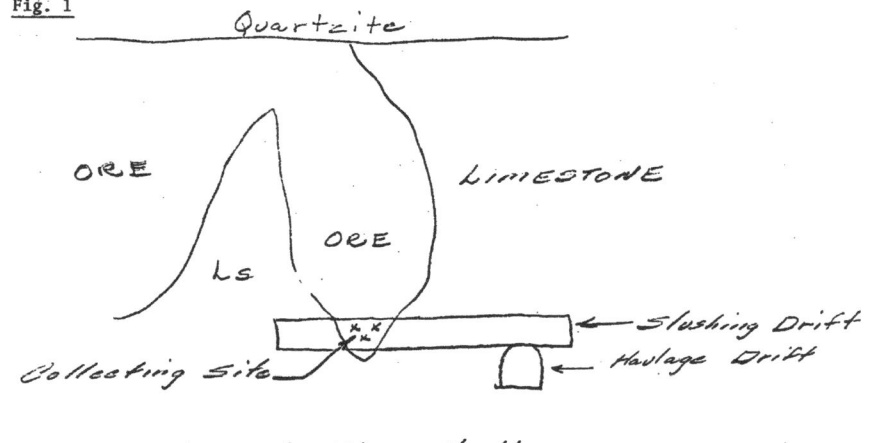

Fig. 1 — Section Looking North

ZEOLITES AT CORNWALL, PA.

Recently the Bethlehem Mines Corporation has been removing the upper strata of limestone and "blue conglomerate" from their East End Ore Body. This southeast extension of the old pit has revealed some minerals in the "blue conglomerate" not reported to date. Included in this group are the zeolites: heulandite and chabazite. Dr. Arthur Montgomery or Lafayette College has confirmed this information and adds that thomsonite has been found also.

Other zeolites included in the recent "blue conglomerate" findings are stilbite and natrolite. The stilbite has been found in the common sheaf arrangements and some as more-rare singular bladed crystals about 1/4" x 1/4" x 1/32" in size. The natrolite is present as a dense white massive mineral and as fine hair-like radiating crystals. Some stilbite has very flat terminations on sheaf ends and there are some questions in the writer's mind as to how this happened. There appears to be plenty of open space for the sheaf to terminate in the normal rounded fashion but these appear to have been filed off to a flat or slightly convex surface. Such crystals are associated with chabazite.

Other zeolites have been found in the diabase at Cornwall. Apophyllite occurs in thin tabular crystals. These crystals form rosettes in some instances. Pseudocubical or long and square prismatic type apophyllite crystals are also found. Natrolite is associated with analcite and apophyllite and has been found in sizes from pencil lead to hair thickness. Some laumontite of microscopic size is present with analcite.

Milt Leet
Mining Engineer
Cornwall, Pa.

APPENDIX

1. A Slice of Life

2. Housing a Collection

3. Money and Minerals

4. Display Collection Inventory 2023

5. My World of Microminerals

6. Collecting Crystallized Minerals

7. Wonder of Discovery

Our move to Louisville in 1991 gave me some incentive to thin out my collection. This 40-pound specimen of magnetite with antigorite was collected from Grace Mine in Morgantown PA. I donated it to the Pennsylvania State Museum in Harrisburg. — MLL

A SLICE OF LIFE

Written Late 1960s

My interest in minerals goes back to 1950 when a friend presented me with some stones from the Lake Superior shores. The different colors and smooth surfaces were very pretty and interesting to a ten year old boy. We lived in Michigan at that time. I had some close buddies who went with me to the vacant fields around home. There we collected all the colors we could find. This started me on my way to an eventual career in the mineral kingdom.

During the years of 1952 to 1957 our family took vacations traveling through every state from the Mississippi River to the west coast. It was on these trips where I was introduced to the beauty of crystals. My father would stop at every rock shop along our way so I could see what they had to offer. During those six years I spent about $100 for 40 specimens which were placed in a cabinet I received as a Christmas gift at the age of seventeen. Some of the best of the material I had collected joined this living room display. The variety of color has always been the main attraction for me.

From 1958 to 1962 my collection grew to include specimens from Climax, Colorado and Morenci, Arizona while working during summer vacations for mining companies. Those college years my collecting took a back seat to many things. Mineral collecting has never been foremost in my activities, but it has been a constant companion of enjoyment which I have turned to whenever the opportunity existed. Now that I am married to a wonderful girl and have two nice children and a good job, the opportunity to collect minerals occurs again.

Since 1962 I have been employed by Bethlehem Mines Corp. at Cornwall, Penna. Cornwall has a long mining history. It goes back to the mid 1700's and is reported to be the oldest continually operating iron mine east of the Mississippi River. The number of minerals found here list in the 80's according to "Mineral Collecting in Pennsylvania," General Geology Report G-33. I have made up suites for collectors which includes as many as 30 different minerals. But as previously stated, my main interest in minerals is beauty through color and form.

I believe it was 1964 when at No. 4 Mine a sight of rare beauty was uncovered. While driving a drift over fingers, two miners broke into a room of stilbite covered with pyrite. The following day I went to see this golden room. The walls glittered with tiny golden specks covering the tan to brown sheaves of stilbite. Some pyrite was iridescent. This sight is a "once in a lifetime" experience said mineralogist Davis Lapham of the Pennsylvania Geological Survey when he visited a few days later. Some specimens from this room are the best of my collection.

The most spectacular specimen now on display at Cornwall is 2' x 2' and covered with scalenohedral calcite crystals three inches long with a druzy white coating on a matrix of brown stilbite. This was brought to the surface sometime before 1962. The occurrence of stilbite has prompted me to become interested in zeolites and other associated minerals. I think the color and variety of crystal forms in this family are the most beautiful I have ever seen.

It was perhaps twenty years ago that a pump room was cut out of diabase below the open pit in No. 3 Mine. Fortunately this faulted area is still preserved. The room was supported by steel sets but the ribs were not covered. Here today, one can descend 300 feet of ladder into a dark, wet, and slightly musty smelling old pump room. Behind the rusting steel these walls reveal cavities which have been robbed of choice specimens. Cavities, just high enough to allow a man's hand to pass, stretch beyond elbow depth and tease the explorer to reach further. At times ice water is encountered and only short durations of exposure can be withstood. At other times one encounters pockets of fine long needles which penetrate the skin and must later be taken out with a knife. These needles if preserved are white or clear and occur as a spray. Donald Hoff, assistant curator, William Penn Memorial Museum, Harrisburg, Pa., explained their formation as resulting from gases evolving from cracks in the faulted diabase. The mineral is natrolite or mesolite-exact identification has not been made. The presence of calcium indicates mesolite. Optical analysis is necessary to make final determination. Preserving these crystals in their original spray form is nearly impossible. I have only a few in my collection.

Apophyllite, analcite, and laumontite are found associated with these fine crystals. All four minerals can be found on thumbnail specimens and therein lies the beauty. Each mineral crystallizes in different forms. The colors are white and clear with some pink, green, and black coloring due to impurities. I have collected fine specimens up to 4" x 6" in size. It is surprising that collecting is still possible in this area. But when one considers how inaccessible this area is, and the difficulty in extracting a good specimen, it's really not too surprising after all. Today I can expect to find ten nice one-inch to two-inch specimens and three to four 2"x3" specimens after six hours of work. There is real satisfaction in breaking into an open cavity lined with crystals. The most joy comes in feeling deep within this small cavity, the smooth faces of what you know must be something beautiful. After carefully extracting a piece, which usually adheres loosely to the cavity wall, and bringing it into the drab, musty darkness; one has only to shine a light into his hand to reveal the beauty God has worked in this dark underground place.

The most interesting of these minerals is apophyllite. This mineral occurs in the less common tabular crystal form. The thing that makes it even more unique is that these tabular blades have grown in a rosette pattern. Sometime these rosettes are filled to such a degree as to form a round bladed ball. Most rosettes are thumbnail in size; however, I have found some as large as 1-1/2 inches in diameter.

My collection is profiting more now than ever before. But you must admit that I'm in a good position to meet the right people, go to the right places, and collect from a source which is very profitable. Perhaps this article may inspire some ten year old boy to become a mining engineer. You can supply a service vitally needed by the mining industry, meet with people who are interested in geology and mineralogy when they take field trips to your location, and continue a hobby of collecting minerals.

HOUSING A COLLECTION

Specimens may be housed in several ways: display cases (openly visible); closed cabinets (readily accessible); or in boxes (not readily accessible). The choice of housing depends on the owner's <u>resources</u> and <u>purpose</u> for collecting. It is the collector's individual reasons for collecting (purpose) and personal attraction to certain specimens that often determines how much effort and money is put into housing. If collectors own specimens because they are pretty and/or unusual, then they are likely to display them; interesting or educational specimens may be in closed cabinets, while saleable items are likely housed in boxes. Understandably, purpose, desire and resources change over time and so can the manner in which a collection is housed.

Specimen size is also a factor that influences the housing decision. Most collectors have a limitation of space. Naturally, a collection of smaller sized specimens allows for increased variety and numbers. Once the purpose for the collection is determined and space limitations are considered, these guidelines should be used in making specimen selections. This may seem the reverse of the natural inclinations to collect whatever you like and whatever you can get. If you plan to sell or trade them, this philosophy of collecting is fine. But if you have no desire to sell or trade, some discipline is required about the size and number of specimens collected.

A display of similar sized specimens will likely be aesthetically less pleasing than having a variation in size. But to display in a manner most efficient to housing, it is desirable to have specimens the same size. There are several options to consider when the primacy purpose for your collection is to display them. If the display case is only eight inches deep, a mirror back can compensate for the flat appearance of specimens in a straight line. Cases fourteen inches deep allow for more rows of specimens, accommodate size variations more readily, and provide a depth of field more pleasing to the eye. Deeper cases are desirable, but many have serious space problems because they are not accessible from the front. Lighting is also an important factor in creating an appealing display. Inexpensive pole lamps serve the purpose, but overhead spot lighting is best. Interior lighting is seldom adequate. Specimens in a collection that are primarily for general interest or for study need not necessarily be on display, but only readily available for view.

So, lighting is important. Organization is important, too. Compartmentalized drawers serve this purpose quite well. Compartment size will be limited by drawer height. It is difficult to conceive cabinets with drawers to accommodate large, heavy specimens. Those may need to be shelved in the open.

Boxed specimens, collected primarily for sale or trade need storage shelves in a dry area. Often "flats" (tops of beer or soda cases) are used for this purpose. These flats are compartmentalized for each specimen by cardboard boxes which can be ordered to size. The flats are selected to fit as a top and bottom for protection of the specimens. The size of the flat makes it easy to carry. Care should be taken not to stack too many flats on top of each other. Such storage configuration makes accessibility a problem and can lead to damaged specimens. Labeling and identification of the contents of each flat are important.

In conclusion, before you bring that specimen home, consider its purpose and how it will be housed. Do you have a place for it? If not, you have found "leaverite". Yes, leave her right where she is.

MONEY AND MINERALS

Written 11/5/99

I still do not know how to approach this subject of "Money and Minerals". But for some time, I have wanted to write about it. This is a more philosophical dissertation than a quantitative analysis.

Let's say for a start - it is a personal thing. Perhaps something that should not be put into print. But, there is no avoiding it - money enters the picture in every hobby we have. How possessed are you with what you "collect?" Any hobby we have is to be enjoyed. Right? Even if you do not buy minerals, you will spend your time and a certain amount of money to seek out personally collected items.

I suppose the reason for collecting has as much to do with the amount of money that is spent as anything. Some may collect for exercise, fresh air, and the thrill of the find. This is a good economical approach to the hobby. But this approach takes time and as we have heard - time is money. So, what is your time worth? What others are willing to pay you, or is your "free time" worth more? Do you collect so that you may make a display of those minerals for your own appreciation of the hobby? If this is what you want, it takes discipline. You must first decide how much room the display will occupy. Then decide what size would best be collected to fill that display. Then study the material available through self collecting, trade, and purchase and then decide the degree to which your display will be limited. Finally, we must get around to the nasty money.

Set a budget. If you are 10 years old, it may be a $5.00 limit for each specimen. It may be that your budget only allows one purchase per year. It could be that only time is what you feel most comfortable about investing. No matter if it is (time or money - remember they are the same) this investment will take from some other aspect of your life. If you have no one but yourself, then decisions are made more easily. But the older we get, the more we are likely responsible for others besides ourselves, and the more we must weigh the importance of each aspect of our lives.

So, a hobby must be a balanced investment. Some of us are short time investors while others are in hobbies for life. Personally, mineral collecting has been a lifetime pursuit. This article addresses those who have selected mineral collecting as a lifetime pursuit.

When people view my collection, they always ask: "How did you get all those things?" I tell them I collected, traded, and bought them. That answer satisfies them, and it is short enough to be comprehended. But the truth is a much longer response. A response that no one would have the patience to listen to, because there is a whole story behind each specimen. A story of time and money invested by someone.

As a child, your parents may not object to one corner of your room being neatly arranged to display your collection. As an adult, your family may not object to one corner of a room being neatly arranged to display your collection. Notice there is a pattern of consideration of others. In addition to space, there are financial considerations. I mean both time and money. What can you afford: four hours a week or four dollars a week?

As with any investment, it is best to start small. Test the waters. Perhaps you can invest very little for now. But life has a way of changing. Priorities shift and there may be more time and money for your hobby at a later date.

This means you should anticipate growth in your display. If growth is not possible, then surely quality improvement can be sought. The goal is satisfaction. Satisfaction that what you have on display represents the best of what you have been able to collect.

If you collect to impress yourself, you will never be disappointed. Because you alone know the resources available to you. If you collect to impress others, you will never achieve satisfaction. The impression of others is dependent upon their exposure to other collections and not your resources. So, collect to impress yourself. Do not expect others to be equally impressed.

So, what sum of investment is required to impress you? That amount is likely to change over time. The beauty of collecting minerals is that one may always improve upon each specimen. So, the hobby allows us to grow as our resources change. The $5 limits per specimen became $20 per specimen and then $100 per specimen and then a few may be acquired for hundreds of dollars. There are a select number who venture into the thousands of dollars per specimen. No matter what limits you may have now selected for yourself, it should be done in perspective of other life demands.

In summary, Discipline - Discipline - Discipline. There is no getting around it. A collection must be planned. First consideration: how much room to devote? Second consideration: what size and number of specimens to be displayed? Third consideration: how will the display be organized? Fourth consideration: how will the display be arranged? Fifth consideration: how much investment will be made?

In conclusion, we can understand why we never read much about what it takes to have a nice mineral collection. The whole subject is a personal thing. It cannot be quantified. Isn't that a joyful revelation?

DISPLAY COLLECTION INVENTORY 2023

The table below summarizes the collecting activity that produced the display collection as of my most recent inventory in 2023. Some specimens were purchased and some were acquired by trade or gift. I've also summed the amount spent on purchases. These figures in no way reflect the collection's current value, only the amount I have invested in the specimens currently on display.

Specimen Numbers	Years Acquired	Number of Specimens Purchased	Total Cost of Purchases	Number of Specimens Acquired by Trade or Gift
Up to 100	1964 — 1969	6	$35	25
100 to 200	1969 — 1970	3	$9	7
200 to 300	1970 — 1971	1	$3	16
300 to 400	1971	6	$29	18
400 to 500	1972 — 1974	17	$295	10
500s (Part 1)	1974 — 1982	20	$668	5
500s (Part 2)	1982 — 1992	33	$1519	1
600s (Part 1)	1992 — 2000	37	$1746	0
600s (Part 2)	2001 — 2010	28	$1251	5
700s (Part 1)	2010 — 2011	30	$1258	0
700s (Part 2)	2012 — 2019	24	$1403	1
700s (Part 3)	2020 — 2023	13	$1136	0
TOTAL		218	$9352	88

MY WORLD OF MICROMINERALS

Written 8/12/25

After retiring in 1999, I entered the world of microminerals hoping to learn more about a greater variety of minerals. In the process, I discovered 453 different minerals. It was a good feeling. There isn't paper enough to do justice to what was seen, and I certainly do not have the words necessary to describe what I discovered.

After joining a micromineral club in Cleveland, Ohio, I met Tim Barnes in Lexington, Kentucky and was impressed with the way he cataloged his collection. Books were collected and equipment was purchased for viewing. Magazine articles were read from the collection of "Rocks and Minerals" and "The Mineralogical Record" that were kept on shelves in our storage room in the basement.

This award-winning photo reveals beauty the naked eye cannot see.

The really nice thing about collecting micros is the availability of specimens. My objective was to find examples of new minerals. "Fleischer's Glossary of Mineral Species 1999" served as the catalog for what was collected. Micros were so plentiful that others provided specimens at club symposiums. On occasions there were specimens for sale that were of interest, but for my purpose the "freebie" tables provided much desirable material. All I had to do was attend symposiums and my desires were met. For someone who was retired, time was never an issue. This is what is memorable about this hobby.

A collector of micros who provides mounts for their specimens are called micro-mounters. My shaking hands never allowed me to try this activity. I merely affixed the specimen to the bottom of a hinged 1" x 1" plastic box. When viewing under a scope, I just worked with the plastic boxes. Of course, mounting in a clay-like compound and not on tooth picks (like real mounters) is much easier.

Forty plastic boxes were housed in white cardboard boxes. A special cabinet was constructed to house the white boxes. The finished product looked like a bookcase of white boxes. The photograph on the next page shows where I did my work. My stereo microscope with light is in the foreground, and the bookcase with the white boxes is in the back.

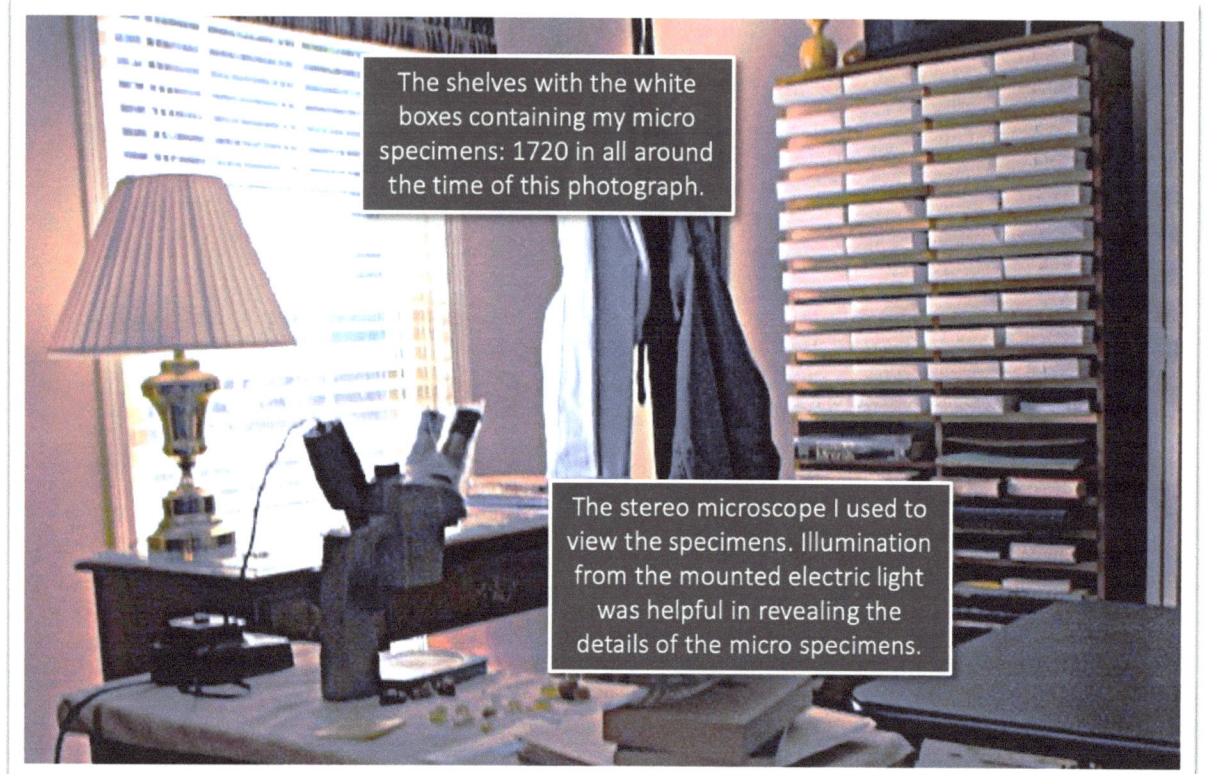

The shelves with the white boxes containing my micro specimens: 1720 in all around the time of this photograph.

The stereo microscope I used to view the specimens. Illumination from the mounted electric light was helpful in revealing the details of the micro specimens.

When the time came to sell my micromineral collection, my documentation of the specimens was as important to the buyer, Tim Barnes, as the specimens themselves. Good documentation of a micromineral collection is essential. Specimen boxes must be numbered and a careful record kept of their contents. The printed inventory of my collection was 35 pages long. I stored it in a 3-ring binder with each page in a clear plastic sleeve.

Crystallography is a challenging science, so instead of trying to name the class and habits of various crystals in my documentation, I focused on colors I saw when viewed under a microscope. I felt that using language most people could understand was important. The micros described in the table at the end of this article came from the Poudrette Quarry, Mont Saint-Hilaire, Quebec, Canada. A location source for each micro was listed along with the specimen number and description.

My time with micros ended at the 2018 summer gathering of the Central U.S. Micromineral Symposium in Clarksville, Indiana on September 13-15. There were 13 people in attendance. I chose the occasion to sell all things related to the hobby. Of the 13 people in attendance at the Central U.S. Micromineral Symposium, five people made purchases: Tim Barnes, Sharon Fox, Jim Stoops, Steven Stuart, and Ron Jackson. Thank you all. Sharon, thanks, too, for connecting me to Ed Weber. Ed purchased my copy of the first edition (1974) of the "Encyclopedia of Minerals". I called it my "Bible". Ed's father's cousin, Julius, was one of the editors of this book.

The collection at that time had 1731 specimens collected over a span of 10 years from 2001 to 2010. These specimens came from 28 sources, and I kept records of the names associated with each of those sources except for symposium finds which numbered 439. In a final review of expenses, I determined my total cost for the

specimens over my collecting years was $1005 and equipment was $846. I spent $465 on books and about $430 on display boxes, bringing my total investment to $2746.

There is no denying it. If your eyes can tolerate the strain, the sight of a crystallized micromineral under a microscope is as rewarding as the macro-minerals. The more you increase the magnification with a good stereo microscope the more you will discover. The experience of seeing completed crystal growth in the mineral world is very satisfying.

Number	Description
647	Synchysite tabular hexagonal xls. Somewhat rounded on corners, grey in color
648	Synchysite use 30x to see grey xls among clear prisms of unknown
649	Taeniolite tan mica plates. See 651 / Carletonite blue
650	Carletonite exhibiting color zoning from blue to pink to white. See front of box for xl.
651	Carletonite exhibiting color zoning from blue to pink to white / Taeniolite tan mica plates
652	Rutile black needles with Quartz
653	Polylithionite tan mica / Albite white / Aegirine black
654	Serandite orange rhombs / Uknown grey rounded waxy balls / Unknown blade bladed xl.
655	Albite white / Unknown milky triangular xls. / Unknown tan blocky xl villiaumite MR v21 p345
656	Arfvedsonite long gray needles / Gmelinite white rosettes / Fluorite / white rounded masses
657	Aegirine / Serandite orange rhombs / Albite white
658	Dawsonite clear with striated faces / Siderite? Golden / Albite chalk white
659	Albite white / Unknown gray needles in cavity @30X

COLLECTING CRYSTALLIZED MINERALS

Written 12/12/21

Why do we do what we do? There are many reasons for collecting and there are many aspects of the mineral world that can provide an individual with fulfillment. Just think of all the activities available to the collector. A person may study, explore, travel, dig, clean, polish, cut, tumble, carve, form jewelry, trade, sell, buy, and display minerals.

Success in collecting minerals is similar to finding a fish. First, know where the fish resides. Go to the lake where the fish has been known to be found. Have the proper tools with you to catch the fish. Know where in the lake the fish is most likely to reside. Instead of dropping a line in the water, start digging and breaking rock. Those who want to be assured of having fish to eat, go to a store and make a selection. Those who want to be assured of a desired mineral specimen, go to a mineral show.

Can a mineral specimen be a friend? It depends on what is expected from a friend. A mineral specimen is a step down from having a dog. But the care you must give a rock is minimal. I wrote a poem about my collection thirty-five years ago. It was entitled: "Friends of Mine" and they still are and always will be friends who are filled with wonder and beauty.

Many mineral specimens are interesting, but relatively few are beautiful. The best show specimens are represented by the following: silicate minerals of quartz, beryls, tourmalines, garnets, and micas. They provide high lusters. Zeolites and their associations provide a variety of crystals in close association.

Carbonates of calcite, aragonite, malachite, azurite, rhodochrosite, and smithsonite are very colorful. Haloids of fluorite come in a variety of colors. Sulfates include celestite, selenite and barite and can be collected in good sized crystals. Oxides and sulfides of iron, lead, and zinc add metallic lusters to crystals. Known also for their color are: vanadinite, crococite, wulfenite, pyromorphite, adamite, and mimetite.

What's it takes to have a nice mineral collection? First and foremost, have money and time. The less money you have, the more time it will take. The best specimens go to the highest bidder or the person who has found the specimen. Are you on a limited budget? Most are. The nice thing about mineral specimens is you can get them at no cost except your time and a little gas money. If you have 65 years to build a collection and you want something colorful, go to mineral shows and shop. As you get older you may have more to spend. You will have more time.

Microminerals provide an excellent opportunity to expand into a greater variety of crystallized minerals. Many minerals cannot be found in any size larger than a few millimeters. Observing these specimens requires magnification of about 10X. The really good thing about this hobby is cost. Collectors provide "freebies" at their meetings. If you are collecting these specimens for an education, the freebie tables are happy hunting grounds. Once you have made the initial investment in a microscope and light, the collecting can be relatively less expensive and very interesting.

People make a difference in the world of mineral collecting. Finding someone who has the same "eye" is a real joy, and there is a great benefit to establishing relationships. These relationships provide opportunities for growth. When you read an article about a famous collector – usually written after their passing – you will see how important other people were to their career. The best collectors do not work alone.

The Wonder of Discovery

I never knew your name, nor the place from which you came.

I never knew you were so bright, when you were buried from the light.

I never knew the color you would be, and it never mattered much to me.

I never knew what made you grow in that world so far below.

I never knew it meant so much to have your "face" to touch.

I never knew I'd find a gem; such a thought was just a whim.

I never knew you would be mine- only something for to pine.

I never knew it could be true until you came into view.

12 December 1999

www.ingramcontent.com/pod-product-compliance
Lightning Source LLC
Chambersburg PA
CBHW041644070526

44586CB00004B/75